The Best of Dr. JAC™

The Best of Dr. JAC™

Joyce Armstrong Carroll

"That is question now;
And then comes answer like an Absey book.
King John, i, 9
Shakespeare

Absey and Company
Spring, TX

Queries regarding rights and permissions should be addressed to:

Absey & Co.
23011 Northcrest
Spring, Texas 77389
281-257-2340

Published by Absey & Co., Spring, Texas
Manufactured in the United States of America

ISBN 1-888842-10-5

T_{able of} C_{ontents}

➤ INTRODUCTION ➤

Why The Best of DR. JAC™?

Since 1991 and the publication of *Picture Books*, first of the five books in the DR. JAC™ series, teachers have hooked students into reading, writing, listening, speaking, viewing, and thinking through the power of books, hands-on experiences, and connections made between artifacts and lessons.

Paradoxical as it may sound, people learn in similar yet unique ways because the neural networks in the human brain work in similar yet unique ways. What teachers rediscovered when using the ideas and activities suggested in the DR. JAC™ books, is that good practice corroborates sound research:
- Learners remember best what they hear first—the primacy effect.
- Learners remember best what they hear last—the recency effect.
- Learners remember best what is new or different—the novelty effect.
- Learners remember best lessons that tap their feelings—the emotional effect.
- Learners remember best what can be connected to life experiences and to prior knowledge—the associative effect.
- Learners remember best what is taught in a context, what has meaning, what makes sense—the contextual effect.

In these six ways learners are similar, so these ways present a constant challenge to the diligent teacher.

Perhaps even more challenging to the act of teaching, however, are the following divergences:
- Learners respond in different ways.
- Learners bring varied experiences, cultures, emotions, moods, knowledge to every lesson.
- Learners language in individual ways, replete with personal connotations, denotations, and inferences.
- Learners mark lessons with their own characteristics that in turn affect the knowing of all learners.
- Learners are influenced by the time of the day, the classroom environment, even the general atmosphere in the school.
- Learners' perceptual discriminations determine what and how they remember.

Since learning is a developmental process, teachers must keep a constant and consistent vigil in order to meet the needs of each student. Teachers have told me that what they like most about the DR. JAC™ series, the reason well-worn copies live on their bookshelves and on their desks, is because the lessons capitalize on the similarity of learners while inviting teachers to capitalize on the singularity of learners.

Teachers also say that they like the ease of following the DR. JAC™ format. The title, author, brief summary, and, in most cases, a suggested grade level for each focal book, helps them make decisions about how to connect the book with lessons, units, themes in their curriculum, other books, or to the objectives mandated on state tests.

Good children's books should be extendable, predictable, and appealing. DR. JAC™ lessons offer extensions that address appropriate skills and tie into various disciplines. Perhaps most rewarding has been the feedback I have received about the artifacts, the tokens that rise out of the book, small mementos that create a connection between the book and the learning.

Several teachers have cited specific instances when artifacts have served as vehicles for review or nudges into further study. For example, before beginning a unit about settling the West, one teacher told me she asked every student to bring a plastic sandwich bag to class. After each story, she gave the students an artifact as a motivation to write about the story, or they crafted an artifact as a way to share their response to the story. Then the students stored their artifacts in their plastic bags. At the end of the unit, the students retrieved each artifact while reviewing specifics about the story from which it came.

Another teacher explained how a simple artifact, a square piece of fabric associated with Patricia Polacco's *The Keeping Quilt*, caused middle school students to make a class quilt and then to research gift-giving wedding customs among various ethnic groups. This, in turn, presented the teacher with the opportunity to introduce symbolism as a literary term in which something means what it is and something more (gold/wealth, flower/love, salt/lives with flavor, the ubiquitous quilt/home).

Even more exciting is how gifted teachers take the idea of the artifact and put their own spin on it. Recently I observed such a teacher, Stephen Shearer, doing just that. Using "Lunch," a poem from the ALA Best Book 1998 by Kathi Appelt called *Just People & Paper/Pen/Poem*, he galvanized a group of tough twelfth graders into reading, talking, brainstorming, and drawing as a form of prewriting. Then came the artifact. Every student received a plain brown paper bag filled with three pieces of candy and five writing prompts. The bags were folded at the top in the manner of a lunch bag. Shearer delivered each bag but cautioned the students to wait for his signal before opening their bags. The students, some big and seemingly disinterested in their black leather jackets, some insecurely slumped low in their seats, others playing the cool dude or the distracted sophisticate, became like little kids eager to see their prize, eager to open the bag, eager. After that, getting them to choose one of the prompts to write about simply became the thing to do.

In keeping with the research, Shearer and others like him have used DR. JAC™ lessons as models for ways to unite learners with learning by:
- giving sound but exciting ways to begin and end lessons,
- providing novel ideas to motivate the learners,

- making clear connections to prior knowledge and experiences,
- furnishing fun ways to link learning with the emotional brain,
- suggesting related books and ways to use them—

all within the meaningful context of the focal book and subsequent writing. Additionally, every lesson suggests a publishing event.

Invitations and challenges issued in DR. JAC™ lessons, which are also built upon research, help teachers tap individual differences among students. Students use their own resources to express their knowing in ways that help them make sense of the learning, while teachers use their own resources to validate those responses. Collaborative techniques and sharing strategies enrich lessons and classroom environments since students are encouraged to display their work in myriad ways that support ownership and shout that school is a place where they are reflected, that school is a place where they belong.

Unfortunately, though, because books go out of print, some of the focal books in each DR. JAC™ have become difficult to find. Hence, I have extrapolated the children's books that are still in print from the five original DR. JAC™'s and compiled those lessons into one source—*The Best of DR. JAC™* .

Coda: While conducting a workshop for a regional educational service center, I noticed teachers passing a book around at break, smiling, nodding, taking notes, and passing the book on. Curious, I positioned myself for a better look. To my delight, it was *Story Books*, the second in the DR. JAC™ series, published in 1992 but apparently still alive in 1998. That episode provided just the impetus I needed to undertake this project. It reminded me of a wish I once read, its author lost in the haze of memory, "May our hearts and minds explode as we teach and learn together."

The Best of Picture Books

Brown Bear, Brown Bear, What Do You See?

Bill Martin Jr.

Holt, Rinehart & Winston, 1983

Grade level: Pre-K-2

Artifact: A healthy honey treat (see Science Connections) or a gummy bear.

Summary: On page after page students see a variety of colorful animals and one mother looking at them.

READING/WRITING CONNECTIONS

1. Read the title and author. Show the basic parts of the book: cover, dust jacket, spine, pages.
2. Read the book and share the pictures, while inviting students to talk about what they see.
3. Reread the book and invite the students to participate in a rhythmic reading of each page.
4. Have students imitate the sounds and movement appropriate to each animal.
5. Show a stuffed bear. Make up and tell its story. Invite students to share stories about their favorite bears.
6. Distribute gummy bears and invite students to write about their favorite bears.

EXTENSIONS

 VOCABULARY/SPELLING:

brown	black	gold	red	yellow
blue	green	purple	white	

LIBRARY CONNECTIONS

1. Research:
   Read and look at bear books, such as *The Little Polar Bear* series by Hans de Beer

and non-fiction books about bears.

2. Corpus of work by an author, co-author, illustrator:
   Check *An Author a Month (for Pennies)* by Sharron L. McElmeel for more information on the author and additional ideas for this book. Show other books by Martin and explain the concept of a coauthor by discussing Martin's coauthor John Archambault. Explore the similarities and differences among books.

3. Discuss the artwork of Ted Rand. Compare and contrast Rand's artwork to that of Eric Carle. Compare the artwork of James Endicott in *Listen to the Rain* to that of Rand and Carle.
   ✤ *Barn Dance*
   ✤ *The Ghost-Eye Tree*
   ✤ *Here Are My Hands*
   ✤ *Knots on a Counting Rope*
   ✤ *Listen to the Rain*
   ✤ *Up and Down on the Merry-Go-Round*
   ✤ *White Dynamite and Curly Kidd*

4. Literary appreciation:
   Create a book and bear corner. Display Martin and Archambault's books along with other bear favorites, including the classic *The Story of the Three Bears* or *Goldilocks and the Three Bears* (usually attributed to Robert Southey) . Others might include *A Bear Called Paddington* by Michael Bond and its sequels; A. A. Milne's *Winnie the Pooh* and *House at Pooh Corner*, Marjorie Flack's *Ask Mr. Bear*; Else Minarik's *Little Bear*. Add bear calendars and posters. Invite students to bring in their stuffed bears and arrange them around the books.

6. Focus on bears by showing other books about bears:
   ✤ Marta Koci's *Sarah's Bear* tells the adventures of a teddy bear.
   ✤ Brinton Turkle's *Deep in the Forest* wordlessly shows a switch on "Goldilocks."
   ✤ Marjorie Weinman Sharmat's bear in *I'm Terrific* learns a valuable lesson.
   ✤ David McPhail's *The Bear's Toothache* solves a big bear's problem.
   ✤ David McPhail's *Fix-It* tells of replacing television with books for Emma.
   ✤ David McPhail's *First Flight* tells about a teddy bear's first airplane flight.
   ✤ Frank Asch's *Skyfire* explains what Bear does when he first sees a rainbow.
   ✤ Bernard Waber's *Ira Sleeps Over* proves that even big kids love teddy bears.
   ✤ Jane Hissey's *Old Bear* tells how Old Bear's friends rescue him.

 SCIENCE CONNECTIONS

1. Hibernation:
   Cover a refrigerator box with brown papier mâché to look like a cave. Students may "hibernate" as they read their chosen bear books or write or draw about bears.

2. Healthy Honey:
   Make healthy honey treats by mixing honey and peanut butter. Put teaspoonsful of the mixture in tiny cups. Give each child a sesame stick and let them eat honey like bears.

SOCIAL STUDIES CONNECTIONS

1. Bear's Habitats:
   Locate on a map places where bears live, such as wilderness areas and national parks.
2. Map making:
   Let students draw freehand maps. They identify places where they think bears would live by pasting on bear stickers or stamping the areas with a bear stamp.

 DRAMA CONNECTIONS

Rhythmic activity:
Gather the students in a circle. All bend over at the waist as they recite, "Brown Bear, Brown Bear, what do you see?" A child, designated as first, stands up straight and responds by calling up another bear he or she has *researched*. For example, "I see a polar bear looking at me." All bend again, this time asking, "Polar Bear, Polar Bear, what do you see?" The next child responds and so on around the circle. Repeats, colors, numbers, and fantasy bears are acceptable.

 ART CONNECTIONS

1. Bear-bag name places:
   Cut a brown shopping bag down the fold at each corner to the bottom. Draw a bear's head in one wide side section, a body in the section that was the bottom of the bag, legs in the other wide side section, and arms in the narrow side flaps. Have students write their names across the bear's chest. Girls put a red paper bow on the bear's head; boys at the bear's neck.
2. Decorated bear folders:
   Have students decorate folders to hold all their bear work.

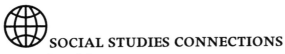 PUBLISHING

Each child's bear sits in his or her chair for PARENTS OPEN HOUSE, holding the folder containing all the child's work in its lap.

2

When the Clay Sings

Byrd Baylor
Illustrated by Tom Bahti

Aladdin Books, 1972
Caldecott Honor Book,
ALA Notable Book

Grade level: All levels

Artifact: Pottery shards (buy cheap pots to break,
or obtain from a potter, or the art department)

Summary: This book, rich in design and language, leads all readers to recognize "that every piece of clay is a piece of someone's life" by looking at the designs of prehistoric American Southwest pottery, as discovered by contemporary American Indian children. Some find shards and listen to the voices; some find pieces that fit together to tell stories; some find whole bowls that beg for dramatic play.

READING/WRITING CONNECTIONS

1. Either in or outside the classroom, strategically place bits of pottery.
2. Read aloud, stopping at places such as, "They say that every piece of clay is a piece of someone's life," or "They even say it has its own small voice and sings in its own way." Explore what students think those sentences mean.
3. Invite students to embark on a pottery hunt. When they find a piece of clay, they are to hold it, study it, listen to its voice, and figure out its creator's life. Discuss their ideas.
4. Have students write about and share what they discovered in their clay.

EXTENSIONS

 VOCABULARY/SPELLING:

ancient	bowl	wide-eyed	whisper
Indian	pretend	deerskin	feather
blanket	language	speckled	costumes
thousand	polishing	cliffhouse	flute
whirlwinds	skinny	fierce	medicine
fierce	wrestling	mountain	canyon
lizards	antelope	lion	wildcats

 LIBRARY CONNECTIONS

1. Awards:

   Discuss the Caldecott and the American Library Association awards. Older students can research these awards: criteria for awarding, year they began, and a sampling of books that have received these awards.

2. Corpus of work by an author:

   Gather other books by Baylor. Look at the artwork by Tom Bahti and Peter Parnall and discuss the style of each.

   ❖ *Amigo*
   ❖ *The Best Town in the World*
   ❖ *The Desert is Theirs* (Caldecott Honor Book)
   ❖ *Everybody Needs a Rock* (ALA Notable Book)
   ❖ *Guess Who My Favorite Person Is*
   ❖ *Hawk, I'm Your Brother* (Caldecott Honor Book)
   ❖ *If You Are a Hunter of Fossils* (Reading Rainbow Selection)
   ❖ *The Way to Start a Day* (Caldecott Honor Book)
   ❖ *Feet!*
   ❖ *I'm in Charge of Celebrations*

3. Research:

   Folklore is sometimes called the "mirror of people." It includes songs, festivals, dances, rituals, stories, and art. Students can research the folklore of the Anasazi, Mogollon, Hohokam, and Mimbres cultures by using reference materials, including atlases, encyclopedias, almanacs, and other reference books.

 SOCIAL STUDIES CONNECTIONS

1. Study the geography and topography of the American Southwest by making "baker's clay" relief maps of this area. To make baker's clay, measure and mix 1 cup flour, 1/2 cup salt, and 2 tsp. cream of tartar. Add 1 cup water, 2 Tbsp., oil, 2 tsp. vanilla extract, and 8-15 drops of food coloring, if desired. Heat. Stir over high heat about 3 minutes or until the "dough" clumps into one huge ball and "cleans" the pan's sides. Cool. Knead out any lumps. Store in airtight containers for future use or sculpt into relief maps immediately.

2. Study the American Southwest Indians:

   Have students examine the art designs on the pottery of the Anasazi, Mogollan, Hohokam, and Mimbres cultures of Arizona, New Mexico, Utah, and Colorado. Compare and contrast with designs found in the caves of France and Spain. Use books such as Keith Brandt's *Indian Crafts* and *Indian Homes* for younger students. All levels may create a paper border for the classroom of designs discovered during their research.

3. Discuss the word *prehistoric* and introduce the word *archaeological*. Discuss how archaeologists deduce things about ancient peoples from artifacts, just as students did by examining pottery shards.

 ART CONNECTIONS

1. Field trip:

   Take a field trip to a museum that features Native American Indian art. Use the book *Visiting the Art Museum* by Laurene Krasny Brown and Marc Brown to prepare students for the trip; pages 31-32, "Tips for Enjoying an Art Museum," are particularly good.

2. Create an exhibit:

   Set up an area where students can display the shards they received as artifacts. Using their imaginations and what they discovered by doing research, have students write a card to accompany each shard, giving an approximate date and cultural source. Younger students might imagine where the shard came from, give a name to its place of origin, and provide a date.

3. Create Indian designs:

   Distribute large pieces of sepia-colored paper. Have students work together in groups to make a mural with Indian designs, following Bahti as a model.

 MUSIC CONNECTIONS

1. Write the chant:

   Share a chant such as "A Chant Out of Doors" by Marguerite Wilkinson (in *Bluestone*). Ask students to join in a second reading.

2. Divide students into groups to research, write, and perform a group chant. They may also model Paul Fleischman's *I Am Phoenix : Poems for Two Voices* or *Joyful Noise: Poems for Two Voices* to create and perform chants for two voices or groups.

 PUBLISHING

Small groups may create a part of a CLASS BOOK ON CHANTS, using as a model *Dancing Teepees: Poems of American Indian Youth* (poems selected by Virginia Driving Hawk Sneve, with art by Stephen Gammell).

The Blue Balloon

Mick Inkpen

Little, Brown, 1989

Grade level: 1-5

Artifacts: Balloons or balloon stickers

Summary: Through pages that open in various ways, the reader "sees" as the little boy blows up a wonderful balloon that never bursts, despite being stretched, squeezed, squashed, whacked, run over, and let fly.

READING/WRITING CONNECTIONS

1. Give students a balloon apiece and invite them to imitate the actions of the narrator as you read along. (Have extra balloons on hand, as real balloons *will* burst!)
2. Lead students through a mapping of the book. Begin with the book's title and brainstorm words.
3. Have students write and illustrate about their own balloons.

Making a Balloon Book

Show a model of an eight-page book and demonstrate how to make an eight-page *Prewriting Balloon Book*:

• Fold an 8-inch by 11 1/2-inch piece of paper in half, short end to short end, and crease.

• Fold back one side half way and crease; fold back the other side halfway and crease. (If opened fully, the paper would be creased in four long rectangles.)

• Keeping the paper folded, fold it short end to short end and crease. (If opened fully, the paper would have eight rectangles.)

• Unfold the last fold and allow the sides to flip down. (The center fold will look like a tent peak; the paper can stand by itself on a desk or a table.)

• Rip carefully or cut down from the peak of the tent where the center folds meet. Cut only down to the next fold.

• Pick the paper up with one hand on either side of the cut. Fold down so the cut is

across the top. You will need to recrease one fold.
- Fold into the shape of a book.

Prewriting in the Books

1. Invite the students to use their eight-page books for prewriting a story about balloons, using the following pattern.
   - Page 1 or Cover—Write your name. They may return to title it or add a design later.
   - Page 2—Write adjectives that describe balloons.
   - Page 3—Write verbs (action words) that tell what balloons do or what can be done with balloons.
   - Page 4—Write adverbs that apply to how balloons do what they do.
   - Page 5—Pretend you are talking to a friend about your balloon. What would you say? Write down that dialogue.
   - Page 6—Write what your balloon is like or unlike.
   - Page 7—Write what your balloon might say if it could talk.
   - Page 8—List some ideas for a story about your balloon.
2. Talk about each page first in order to encourage oral responses as examples. Using the prewriting books for ideas, have students write stories about their balloons in another eight-page book.

EXTENSIONS

 VOCABULARY/SPELLING:

soggy	shiny	squeaky	whacked
ordinary	balloon	squashed	indestructible

 LIBRARY CONNECTIONS

1. Research:
   Encourage students to find books with unusual construction and share their discoveries with classmates.
   ✤Mitsumasa Anno's *Peekaboo* has moveable paper hands in front of faces.
   ✤Eric Carle's *Papa, Please Get the Moon for Me* has pages that fold out.
   ✤Eric Carle's *The Secret Birthday Message* has a code which cut pages uncover.
   ✤Harriet Ziefert and Mavis Smith's *In a Scary Old House* has fold-out pages.
   ✤Bradman & Chamberlain's *Look Out, He's Behind You!* is a lift-the-flap book.
   Students share their book "finds" with classmates.
2. The making of books:
   Study Aliki's *How a Book is Made*.

SCIENCE CONNECTIONS

1. Air power:

   Show how to lift a book without touching it. Put a balloon on a table so its opening hangs over the table edge. Put a book on top of the balloon. Raise the book by blowing up the balloon. Discuss how air under pressure can move heavy objects.

2. Static electricity:

   Show how to stick a balloon on a wall. Take a blown-up balloon and rub it against something woolen or against hair. Put the balloon against a wall and let it stick. Discuss how the balloon became charged.

SOCIAL STUDIES CONNECTIONS

1. Research on balloons:
   - Find out why and when people send balloons as gifts.
   - Look up Charles Goodyear and then report to the class what he discovered.
   - Look up the history of balloons to find when they were first used and who used them.

2. Sources of rubber:
   - Read about how rubber is extracted from trees and plants.
   - Locate on a map the lands that grow rubber trees and plants.
   - Read about these lands.

ART/LANGUAGE ARTS CONNECTIONS

1. Making "rubber maps":

   Draw a map of India, Malay, or another rubber-producing place. Affix tiny rubber objects such as erasers and rubber bands to the map and list the many uses of rubber in the map's margins. Write about rubber and its many uses.

2. Make another eight-page book:

   Using the dictionary, find at least six words that have the word rubber in them (for example: rubberneck). Illustrate one word on each page of the book and write something funny for each.

PUBLISHING

Display the writings, drawings, maps, and books around an old tire. Include nonfiction books about rubber. Call the display THE RUBBER WORKS.

The Important Book

Margaret Wise Brown

Harper & Row, 1949

Grade level: All levels

Artifact: An accordion book

Summary: Through the cadence of language, this book stimulates the senses and awareness of what is important about everyday, mundane things such as a spoon, a daisy, a shoe, as well as about self.

READING/WRITING CONNECTIONS

1. After introducing the book, read about the cricket, calling attention to the parenthetical statement "(you tell me)." Explain the cadence of the book and invite students to join in as you read.
2. Together compose an *important* page. Use the inside cover and title-page suggestion of *glass* as the starter.
3. Compose a page aloud for each of the other objects on the inside cover and title page.
4. Choose an object in the room as the subject of a composition using the same cadence as the book.
5. Students are now ready to compose on their own. Ask them to think of something important they could describe using the same cadence as the book.
6. Show students how to make an accordion book:
   • Fold a paper in half.
   • Fold one side back halfway.
   • Fold the other side back halfway. The accordion book will thus have a cover and seven long, narrow pages (counting both the front and back of the paper).
7. On the cover, students write *"The important thing about _____ is that _____."* On pages one through six, they write a different description, each not quite as important as the one on the cover. On panel seven, they simply write the word *BUT*.
8. Because the cover and page eight of an accordion book are the same, the book becomes recursive, emphasizing the **important thing**.

EXTENSIONS

 VOCABULARY/SPELLING:

cadence   shovel   hollow   ticklish   crystal   tender

 LIBRARY CONNECTIONS

1. Main idea/ main plot and secondary ideas and subplots:
   Students apply this cadence to pieces of literature by using an accordion book to extract the main idea or main theme and the subthemes or subplots. For example, high school students studying *Macbeth* might work up an accordion book like this:
   * Cover: *The important thing about <u>Macbeth</u> is that the play is about ambition.*
   * Page one: *It is true that the play also deals with guilt.*
   * Page two: *It also tells about delusion.*
   * Page three: *It shows the many facets of despair.*
   * Page four: *It includes weakness and conflict.*
   * Page five: *It emphasizes torment and pathos.*
   * Page six: *Still, it contains elements of courage, loyalty, and imagination.*
   * Page seven: *BUT*
   * Page eight: [Page eight is the cover: Same as "Cover" above.]
   Students may then elaborate on each page's statements.

2. Corpus of work by an author:
   Gather other books by Brown. Display in the Author's Corner.
   ✤*The City Noisy Book*
   ✤*David's Little Indian*
   ✤*The Dead Bird*
   ✤*Goodnight Moon*
   ✤*The Little Fisherman*
   ✤*The Little Island* (written under her pseudonym Golden MacDonald)
   ✤*The Runaway Bunny*

 SCIENCE CONNECTIONS

Making a main hypothesis:
Students follow the same cadence working with an experiment. (See *More Science Secrets* by Judith Conaway and Renzo Barto.)

* Cover: *The important thing that will make this experiment on growing plants work is the sun.*
* Page one: *It is true you need six clear plastic cups.*

- Page two: *It is also true you need paper towels.*
- Page three: *It requires water.*
- Page four: *It needs masking tape.*
- Page five: *It needs a pen.*
- Page six: *It needs a paper clip.*
- Page seven: *BUT*
- Page eight: [Page eight is the cover: Same as "Cover" above.]

 ## SOCIAL STUDIES CONNECTIONS

Supporting a main idea:
Students follow the cadence to support a main idea, changing *But* to *SO*.

- Cover: *The important thing about George Washington was that everything during his eight-year term of office was a first.*
- Page one: *He was the first president of the United States.*
- Page two: *He was married to the first First Lady.*
- Page three: *He authorized the first U. S. Census.*
- Page four: *Under Washington, we had the first U.S. Mint.*
- Page five: *He convened the first session of the Supreme Court.*
- Page six: *He announced the first official Thanksgiving.*
- Page seven: *SO*
- Page eight: [Page eight is the cover: Same as "Cover" above.]

 ## PUBLISHING

Display students' "important" accordion books around Margaret Wise Brown's *The Important Book*. Juxtapose appropriate objects and other books with their books. Call the display IMPORTANCE!

Chicka Chicka Boom Boom

Bill Martin, Jr. and John Archambault

Simon and Schuster, 1989

Grade Level: Pre-K-2

Artifact: A letter of the alphabet made from felt

Summary: Personified letters of the alphabet climb a coconut tree accompanied by a rhyming, rhythmic chant.

READING/WRITING CONNECTIONS

1. Introduce the book and invite predictions about the book.
2. Show the inside covers of the book. Again invite students to make predictions about the book.
3. Read the book in a rhythmic, chanting way.
4. Reread the book and ask the students to join in the chant.
5. Distribute individual letters of the alphabet made of felt to individual students.
6. Explain that when "their" letter is read from the book, they are to put that letter on a coconut tree which you have made out of felt, glued to a larger piece of felt, and laid on the floor.
7. Read the first part of the book again as the students place their letters on the tree. When you come to "The whole alphabet up the—Oh, no!" mix up all the letters by shaking the "tree."
8. As you read the second part, students retrieve their letters. Reread as appropriate.
9. Allow students to tape their letters onto something in the room that begins with that letter (for example, **C** on the closet, **B** on a book).

EXTENSIONS

 VOCABULARY/SPELLING

coconut   alphabet   tangled   knotted   looped   stooped

 **LIBRARY CONNECTIONS**

1. Different alphabet books:

   Show students several alphabet books, such as:

   ✤ *A is for Angry* by Sandra Boynton

   ✤ *Action Alphabet* by Marty Newmeir and Byron Glaser

   ✤ *C is for Curious* by Woodleigh Hubbard

   ✤ *The Z was Zapped* by Chris Van Allsburg

   Compare and contrast these books to *Chicka,* noting similarities and differences.

2. Corpus of work by an author:

   (See Dr. JAC 1).

 SCIENCE CONNECTIONS

1. Coconut trees:

   • Show students pictures of coconut trees.

   • Point out the texture of their bark and the characteristic shapes of palm leaves.

   • Compare the leaves of the coconut tree to the leaves of other trees, as found in another ABC book called *A B Cedar: An Alphabet of Trees* by George Ella Lyon. Using Lyon's book as a model, have students create a page about the coconut tree.

2. Coconuts:

   • Bring in several coconuts. Let students feel their texture, look at their shape, tell what they look like.

   • Drain the liquid from one as the students watch. (You will probably need a hammer and ice pick to punch through the "eyes" to drain the coconut.) This is "coconut milk." Other products from coconuts are coconut cream and coconut oil.

   • Give students a tiny taste of coconut. Talk about what it tastes like. Discuss things made from coconut.

3. The coconut crab:

   Tell students about the coconut crab, a large land crab that lives in the South Pacific and eats coconuts. Students can draw pictures of what they think this crab might look like.

 SOCIAL STUDIES CONNECTIONS

   Where coconut trees grow:

   • Find the South Pacific on a map of the world or on a globe. Call attention to the islands in that area and teach students what makes a body of land an island.

   • Generally talk about that area: its climate, its people, its culture.

   • Have students find out all the products that come from coconut trees.

 **ART CONNECTIONS**

1. Making coconut trees:
   Give students white paper, a piece of brown burlap, and two different colors of green felt for making coconut trees. (Posters of *Chicka Chicka Boom Boom* are available through Silver Burdett & Ginn. These make a wonderful display, and students can use them as a visual model.)

2. Creating leaf collages:
   Give each child a large green piece of construction paper cut in the shape of a palm leaf to use as a base for a collage of other leaves they find.

3. Cutting and pasting islands:
   Give each child a large piece of blue construction paper and a small piece of brown construction paper. Students cut out an island from the brown paper and paste it on the blue paper. Encourage them to draw coconut trees and coconut crabs on their island.

 PUBLISHING

Students make their own ABC books, either alone or in groups, following ideas gleaned from the books they have read. Advanced students may vary their books by adding a bit of logical thinking and using as their model *Q is for Duck* by Mary Elting and Michael Folsom. Display. Call display WE KNOW OUR ABC's!

Eating the Alphabet

Lois Ehlert

Harcourt Brace Jovanovich, 1989

Grade Level: Pre-K–2

Artifact: Miniature plastic fruits or vegetables or real fruits and vegetables (as described in Science Connection 3).

Summary: This book provides a journey through the alphabet by way of the names and colorful pictures of fruits and vegetables.

READING/WRITING CONNECTIONS

1. Ask students to identify the fruits and vegetables on the cover and invite predictions.
2. Show the title page and discuss the funny face pictured there.
3. Read the book, inviting response to the letters and pictures.
4. Distribute the artifacts and have students identify them.
5. Ask students to write a page about their fruits or vegetables.

EXTENSIONS

 VOCABULARY/SPELLING:

title   introduction   glossary   fruit   vegetable

 LIBRARY CONNECTIONS

1. The Introduction:

   Read the book's introduction. Generally talk about introductions and then have students introduce themselves to the whole class and to a single classmate. Talk about why people and books need introductions.

2. The Glossary:

   Show the book's glossary. Explain the function of a glossary and read some interesting excerpts.

3. Corpus of work by an author:

Gather other books by Ehlert and create a Lois Ehlert Author's Corner. Help students know where to find Ehlert's books in the library.

   ✤ *Color Farm*
   ✤ *Color Zoo* (Caldecott Honor Book)
   ✤ *Feathers for Lunch*
   ✤ *Fish Eyes: A Book You Can Count On*
   ✤ *Growing Vegetable Soup*
   ✤ *Planting a Rainbow*

You may want to include books illustrated by Lois Ehlert, such as *Chicka Chicka Boom Boom*

4. Research:

On the copyright page, Ehlert quotes Anthelme Brillat-Savarin's saying, "Tell me what you eat, and I will tell you what you are." In the reference section of the library, show students how to find books of quotations and share some of the interesting quotations found therein.

 SCIENCE CONNECTIONS

1. Learning about fruits and vegetables:

Use this book to reinforce letter recognition while teaching the identity of various fruits and vegetables.

2. Classifying fruits and vegetables:

Divide students into groups. Give each group stylized, colored-paper replicas of the fruits and vegetables in the glossary and have them paste pictures under one of the headings on a chart labeled "FRUITS," "VEGETABLES," and "FRUITS AND VEGETABLES." They may check the book as they work.

3. Preparing fruits and vegetables:

Under careful supervision allow students to prepare some fruits and vegetables to be eaten. They may cut carrots, apples, bananas, celery, tomatoes. An alternative is to bring fruits and vegetables that may be prepared without cutting such as sectioned oranges, tangerines, or grapefruits; stemmed cherries or grapes; leaves of lettuce or watercress; or pieces of cauliflower or broccoli.

If your budget permits, give each child a berry of some kind, and try to get something unusual to share with the students, such as star fruit, ugli fruit, or jicama.

 SOCIAL STUDIES CONNECTIONS

1. Map making:

Have students choose a country that produces fruits or vegetables. After they have drawn a map of that country, they can research and draw in the fruits and vegetables that come from there. For example, if they chose Mexico, they would draw in an avocado, a jalapeno, jicama, and zucchini.

2. Christopher Columbus:

Help students trace the route Columbus took when he brought corn to Europe from the West Indies.

 ART CONNECTION

Fruit and vegetable faces:

Using the model on the title page, make faces using stylized cut-out or drawn fruits and vegetables.

 MUSIC CONNECTION

Sing and skip to "Oats, Peas, and Beans," from *Go In and Out the Window* , music arranged and edited by Dan Fox .

 PUBLISHING

After students write stories about their fruit and vegetable faces, display the art and the stories emerging from a large cornucopia. Intersperse with artificial fruits and vegetables. Call the display THE FRUITS OF OUR LABOR.

The Jolly Postman and Other People's Letters

Janet & Allan Ahlberg

Little, Brown and Company, 1986

Grade level: All levels

Artifact: A piece of stationery and an envelope

Summary: A jolly postman delivers appropriate mail to fairy-tale characters.

READING/WRITING CONNECTIONS

1. Begin by brainstorming a list of fairy-tale characters.
2. Ask students, if they were to write one of these characters, which one would it be, why they would choose that one, and what they would say. Discuss.
3. Show them the book and see if they can identify all the characters on the cover. (Even older students will love this book for its punning.)
4. Read through the book. Let the younger students actually take the mail out of the envelopes. Talk about each of the characters and review their stories.
5. Distribute the stationery and envelopes and allow students to write a letter to the storybook character of their choice. Share as each student takes a turn sitting in the Author's Chair.

EXTENSIONS

 VOCABULARY/SPELLING:

porridge   magician   occupant   bungalow   hobgoblin   covens

 LIBRARY CONNECTIONS

1. Introduce other books:

    ✤*A Book of Boxes* by Lura Mason contains pages of boxes which open revealing removable items to delight students.

    ✤*My Presents* written and illustrated by Rod Campbell has wrapped presents with word hints about the contents that can be opened, although the items cannot be removed.

❖ *Letters of Thanks: A Christmas Tale* by Manghanita Kempadoo is a series of letters by a Katherine Huntington to a Lord Gilbert thanking him for each of the gifts of the twelve days of Christmas. This is a great book to use for tone and style.

2. Corpus of work by an author:

Check *Bookpeople: A First Album* by Sharron L. McElmeel for biographical information on the Ahlbergs. Gather books by the Ahlbergs. Discuss ways in which each book is special.

❖ *The Clothes Horse and Other Stories*
❖ *Each Pear Plum*
❖ *Funnybones*
❖ *Jeremiah in the Dark Woods*

3. Share a sampling of other books of and about letters:

❖ *The Best of Dear Abby,* Abigail Van Buren (Andrews & McMeel)
❖ *Ernest Hemingway: Selected Letters 1917-1961.* Carlos Baker, ed. (Scribner's).
❖ *Love Letters: An Anthology.* Antonia Fraser ed. (Knopf).

 LANGUAGE ARTS CONNECTIONS

1. Letter writing:
   • Students write a letter as if it would be sent to the Ahlbergs.
2. Persuasive letters:
   • Write to the Customer Relations Manager or Consumers Affairs Office about a legitimate concern or complaint, using the proper form.
3. Friendly letters:
   • Write a friendly letter to a friend or relative.
4. Other letters:
   • Write to "Dear Abby" or "Miss Manners," or write letters of application, inquiry, or letters to the editor.
5. Letter-writing to literary characters:
   • Make a book of letters following the model of *The Jolly Postman* to literary characters students are studying. For example, they may write to Macbeth, Lady Macbeth, Duncan or to Scout or even Harper Lee. This is best done as a series of letters.
6. Pen Pals:
   • Check *All About Letters* for lists of sources for pen pals.

SOCIAL STUDIES CONNECTIONS

1. History of the U.S. Postal Service:

Send for *All About Letters (revised edition)* from NCTE. This 64-page book, produced by the United States Postal Service in cooperation with the National Council of Teachers of English, contains much interesting and invaluable information on the history of the U.S. Postal Service.

2. History in Letters:

✤ *The Book of Abigail and John: Selected Letters of the Adams Family, 1762-1784* (L. H. Butterfield, Marc Friedlander, and Mary-Jo Kline, eds.).

✤ *The Children of Pride.* (Robert Manson Myers, ed.)

✤ *A Letter to Anywhere* by Al Hine and John Alcorn. This book contains the history of letter writing around the world and over centuries.

✤ *Letters in American History: Words to Remember.* (H. Jack Lang, ed.).

 MUSIC CONNECTIONS

Share books that deal with letters from musicians:

✤ *Letters of Beethoven* (3 vols. Trans. Emily Anderson).

✤ *Letters to a Musical Boy* by Mervyn Bruxner.

✤ *Letters to Horseface: Being the Story of Wolfgang Amadeus Mozart's Journey to Italy, 1769-1770, When He Was a Boy of Fourteen.* F. M. Monjo.

 PUBLISHING

Celebrate a RED-LETTER DAY by displaying all the books about letters and all the students' letters. Give the students letter stickers and letter stamps. (This is more fun to do around Valentine's Day.)

Merry-Go-Round:
A Book About Nouns

Ruth Heller

Grosset & Dunlap, 1990

Grade level: All levels

Artifact: A "noun" (object) pulled out of a bag

Summary: This book provides an aesthetically rhythmic study of nouns.

READING/WRITING CONNECTIONS

1. Hold up an object (a miniature merry-go-round would be ideal but not essential). Give its name. Then give its grammatical name—noun.
2. Ask each student to give the name of the object he or she has pulled from the bag. Reinforce repeatedly that the name of each object being held is a noun.
3. Use the title page to identify the thing (e.g.,horse) and its classification (i.e., noun).
4. Read through the book and let students identify the nouns given on each page. When appropriate (given the grade level and knowledge of the students), have them apply the concepts covered in the book to their objects. For example, when discussing common and proper nouns, suggest that each student try to convert his or her common noun to a proper one (horse—Trigger).
5. Give students paper and colored markers. Let each create a page following Heller's model for the noun he or she has chosen.

EXTENSIONS

 VOCABULARY/SPELLING:

common nouns	proper nouns	abstract nouns	concrete nouns
compound nouns	collective nouns	singular nouns	plural nouns
plural compounds	possessive nouns	determiners	hyphenated

LIBRARY CONNECTIONS

1. Rhythmic reading: Reread the book, stopping at places that invite students to supply the rhyming word.

2. "Readers Theatre of Nouns":

   Using the objects they were given, students work in groups to create a readers theatre presentation, incorporating as many concepts about nouns as they can. See *Readers Theatre for Children* and *Readers Theatre for Young Adults* by Mildred Knight Laughlin and Kathy Howard Latrobe for directions on scripting techniques.

3. Corpus of work by an author:

   Help students find other books written or illustrated by Ruth Heller in the library.
   - ❖*Animals Born Alive and Well*
   - ❖*A Cache of Jewels and Other Collective Nouns*
   - ❖*Chickens Aren't the Only Ones*
   - ❖*The Egyptian Cinderella* text by Shirley Climo
   - ❖*Kites Sail High: A Book About Verbs*
   - ❖*Many Luscious Lollipops: A Book About Adjectives*
   - ❖*Plants That Never Ever Bloom*
   - ❖*The Reason for a Flower*

 SCIENCE CONNECTIONS

1. Nouns in science:

   Distribute large pieces of construction paper. Working in groups, students create a collage of "Nouns in Science." Do not give too many specifics: some may want to accompany words with pictures; others may want to relate their collages to a theme, such as "environment nouns." Challenge students to fill the paper with as many words as possible. See how many the entire class found.

2. Quick Wit--Test Your Brain Power:

   Divide students into groups of two and assign the partners to work up a list of ten nouns used in science that fit all the types Heller discusses, such as compound nouns, plural nouns, collective nouns, etc. Then have two groups face each other in a contest. One group gives a word from their list—for example "fish." The other group responds with something like, "*Fishes* is the plural form of *fish*." or "*Fish* is a singular noun; *fishes* is a plural noun."

 ART CONNECTIONS

Noun plates:

- Take two paper plates of the same size. Using a dictionary, students list nouns around one plate like the numbers on the face of a clock. Designate categories. For example, some students make "Proper Name" plates and other students make "Plural Compound" plates. These become the bottom plate.

• Cut a one-inch wedge in the other plate. Title and decorate this (top) plate in Heller's style. Affix the two plates with a brad or paper fastener so the top plate will rotate easily over the bottom plate.

• With a partner, students drill each other using each other's noun plates.

 MUSIC CONNECTIONS

1. Noun Rap:

   Divide students into groups. Each group prepares a "rap"-style song or chant of Heller's book to share with the class.

2. Background music:

   Divide students into groups. Each group explores different kinds of music to use as background to a reading of Heller's book and explains its choices. Tape the chosen pieces and play during a reading of the book.

 PUBLISHING

Display all work done on nouns using a merry-go-round motif. Call the display WE GO-A-ROUND ABOUT NOUNS!

The Enormous Watermelon

Retold by Brenda Parkes and Judith Smith

Rigby Inc. 1986
(reprinted 1989)

Grade level: Pre-K-1

Artifact: A piece of watermelon

Summary: In this big book, Old Mother Hubbard plants a watermelon seed. When the melon is ready to be picked, it is so enormous that she calls, one by one, other nursery-rhyme characters to help her pick it.

READING/WRITING CONNECTIONS

1. Show students the book and discuss how the story, about a "big," enormous watermelon, is like the oversized book. Talk about watermelons.
2. Ask students to tell you what the woman on the book's cover is doing. Tell them that the woman is Old Mother Hubbard; recite the nursery rhyme to remind them about Old Mother Hubbard and invite them to join in.
3. Read the book. Take advantage of the three-quarter-page format, which hints about the next nursery-rhyme character to appear by encouraging students to examine the clues and predict the character. Reread the book so that students join in on the repetitions and make the predictions with more confidence.
4. Give students pieces of watermelon. After they have eaten, distribute large pieces of construction paper to be folded into thirds. In the top panel, students draw a small green melon shape; in the middle panel they draw a big green melon shape; in the bottom panel they draw a bigger green melon shape. Then they write and share stories about a growing watermelon.

EXTENSIONS

VOCABULARY/SPELLING:

Old Mother Hubbard	Humpty Dumpty	watermelon	Little Miss Muffet
juicy	grew	Jack and Jill	enormous
pulled	Willy Winky	picked	kitchen

 LIBRARY CONNECTIONS

1. Share other big books:
   - Use *Time for Rhyme* illustrated by Marjory Gardner, Heather Philpott, and Jane Tanner to reinforce the nursery rhymes and to permit students to identify some of the characters mentioned in *The Enormous Watermelon*.
   - Use *Hattie and the Fox* by Mem Fox to reinforce shared reading and predicting.

2. Introduce other sequencing books, such as *The Day Jimmy's Boa Ate the Wash* and *Jimmy's Boa and the Big Splash Birthday Bash* by Trinka Hakes Noble.

3. Show students where oversized books are kept in the library. Encourage them to play librarian and read them to their friends.

4. Choral refrain:
   Encourage students to repeat the *grew* and *pulled* refrains by controlling their voices. Teach them to whisper, use their normal voices, then make their voices louder. Call attention to how the print gets bigger when the voices should get louder. Talk about the sounds *gr* and *p*.

5. Check *Fun with Choral Speaking* by Rose Marie Anthony for an entire section on "Mother Goose Rhymes" and *One Potato, Two Potato, Three Potato, Four: 165 Chants for Children* compiled by Mary Lou Colgin, for a wide selection of nursery rhymes. Use *Each Peach Pear Plum* by Janet and Allan Ahlberg to find more nursery rhyme characters.

 LANGUAGE ARTS CONNECTIONS

1. Dialogue:
   Show students the red print and explain that the red print means that Old Mother Hubbard is talking. Read those sections in an Old Mother Hubbard voice.

2. Quotation marks:
   Ask students what moves when you talk. (Lips) Show students the two marks around what Old Mother Hubbard says. Tell the students those two marks are like two little lips. One set of little lips signals when the talking begins; one set signals when the talking ends.

3. Story Mural:
   Tape a long sheet of butcher paper on the wall. Make a section for the title and author, a section for the characters, and a series of horizontal blocks. Then invite students to retell the story as you write what they say in the blocks. When Old Mother Hubbard talks, put the words in "little lips" and write her words in red (or you can let a child go over the quotation marks in red, with lipstick, for instance).

SCIENCE CONNECTIONS

1. Things that grow on vines:
   Brainstorm a list of things that grow on vines. Plant the seeds of a melon and chart what happens. See *Pumpkin Pumpkin* by Jeanne Titherington for a description of a growing gourd.
2. Gourds:
   Watermelons are part of the gourd family. Bring in other species for exhibit.
3. Parts of a watermelon:
   Classify the parts of a watermelon— the skin, rind, its fleshy center, and its seeds.
4. Learn the colors of watermelon:
   Make a "Watermelon Color Chart" of red, pink, yellow, white.
5. Reinforce letters: Use *Eating the Alphabet* by Lois Ehlert (See Dr. JAC 6).

 ART CONNECTIONS

Make papier mâché watermelons of different sizes. Paint some in stripes and some in solid colors of green.

 MUSIC CONNECTIONS

Use *Go In and Out the Window* (music arranged and edited by Dan Fox) for the music, words, and art for many classic nursery rhymes.

 PUBLISHING

Make a WATERMELON PATCH:
With *The Enormous Watermelon* in the center, display all the other books used and work the students have done. Place the papier mâché watermelons around the books and writing. Cut out vines, leaves, and tendrils to arrange in and around the display.

The Book of Shadowboxes: The Story of the ABC's

Laura L. Seeley

Peachtree Publishers, 1990

Grade level: All levels

Artifact: Cereal alphabet letters

Summary: Each letter is introduced through rhythm, rhyme, alliteration, repetition, and items beginning with that letter arranged in a shadowbox.

READING/WRITING CONNECTIONS

1. Begin by showing students a shadowbox. Talk about the objects in the box and discuss the purpose of shadowboxes.
2. Show the cover of the book.
3. Read the delightful dedication and discuss the way Seeley uses language in it: "Buddy, who'll window the panes and candy the canes..."
4. Read the poem that introduces "Shadow." Point out that there will be extra things to see. Name the object and see who can spot it first.
5. Read the book, allowing time for the students to savor its richness.
6. Students then pick a cereal alphabet letter from a bag or bowl and list items that begin with that letter. Then, following Seeley's model, they draw a shadowbox and either write or draw in the items which begin with their letter.
7. After they make their shadowbox, they compose a rhyme to match.
8. Share in small groups or in the AUTHOR'S CHAIR.

EXTENSIONS

 VOCABULARY/SPELLING:

avocado	artichoke	armadillo	alligator	buzzing	bugle
cricket	camel	candle	dinosaur	dalmatian	dolphin
envelopes	eclair	flamingo	french fries	giraffe	gerbil
guitar	genuine	guppies	hyena	horizon	igloo

iguana	jaguar	kookaburra	ketchup	khaki	lizard
leprechaun	leopard	mouse	moose	moustache	musical
nostrils	nickel	octagons	ostrich	pepperoni	pelican
quarrels	quivering	rascally	rustic	raisins	sneaky
shovel	teepee	toucan	urn	ukulele	unkempt
urchin	umbrella	versatile	vulnerable	voracious	vitamins
walrus	whispering	whiskers	saxophone	pixies	tuxedo
yuccas	yacht	yogurt	yodeling	zeppelin	zebu

 LIBRARY CONNECTIONS

1. Share other alphabet books.
2. Share antique alphabet books:

   ✤*A: Apple Pie: An Old Fashioned Alphabet Book* by Kate Greenaway delights all ages.

   ✤"An Alphabetical Arrangement of Animals for Little Naturalists" and "The Alphabet of Goody Two Shoes" in *A Treasury of Illustrated Children's Books : Early Nineteenth-Century Classics from the Osborne Collection* by Leonard De Vries helps students see the alphabet from a historical perspective.

 SCIENCE CONNECTIONS

1. Share *Animalia* by Graeme Base for reinforcement of the alphabet as well as the beauty of the animal illustrations.
2. Have students make an ABC book of animals they are studying.

 LANGUAGE ARTS/ART CONNECTIONS

1. Egg-carton shadowboxes:
   Each student makes a shadowbox by putting objects that begin with his or her designated letter in the egg compartments. They may write a rhyme and affix it to the lid.
2. Spatter-paint letters:
   Cut out a letter from cardboard and tape it on a paper plate. Put newspaper around the work area. Dip a toothbrush in tempera paint and run it back and forth over a small piece of screen held above the plate. When the paint dries and the letter is removed from the plate, it will appear in silhouette.
3. Alliteration, Adjectives, Adverbs:
   Use *The Book of Shadow Boxes* as an introduction to the poetic device of alliteration. ("A Kettle's for the kitchen" in *Sing a Song of Popcorn* selected by Beatrice Schenk de Regniers, is also good for alliteration.)

 SOCIAL STUDIES CONNECTIONS

Use the *ABC: The Wild West Buffalo Bill Historical Center Cody, Wyoming* by Florence Cassen Mayers, which illustrates each letter of the alphabet with one or more objects from the Buffalo Bill Historical Center. Students can make an ABC book of artifacts, objects, and people from any period in history with a brief explanation included on each page. They may do the same for their own classrooms. These can be "leather-bound" to give an authentic look:

• Paste small pieces of masking tape every which way over one side (the outer side) of two pieces of very stiff cardboard.

• Use some fabric scraps as wipes to spread tan, brown, or black paste shoe polish over the tape. Wipe away excess and let stand overnight.

• Cover the other side, the inside, of the cardboard with some decorative paper;

• Put the alphabet pages inside and affix with tape, staples, or chicken rings (plastic rings, available from feed stores, which are used to tag chickens).

 PHYSICAL EDUCATION CONNECTIONS

Use *A My name is ALICE* by Jane Bayer to reinforce the alphabet and to work with motor skills (directions given by author at the book's conclusion).

PUBLISHING

Display all the alphabet books and the students' work around and in an enlarged shadowbox which can be constructed with cardboard on the bulletin board or on a table. Call the display, SHADOW OUR LETTERS.

The Best
of
Story
Books

11

Dr. JAC

Sylvester and the Magic Pebble

William Steig

Simon and Schuster, 1969
(Caldecott Winner)

Grade level: All levels

Artifact: A small stone or a colored glass pebble

Summary: When Sylvester finds a shiny red pebble to add to his collection, he discovers its magic power to make wishes come true. By story's end, Sylvester learns to be careful when making a wish.

READING/WRITING CONNECTIONS

1. Read and discuss the story.
2. Produce a pouch or box and invite predictions about its contents.
3. When they guess "magic pebbles" (or, if you prefer, "wish pebbles"), invite talk about wishing. When do we wish? What do we wish for? Do all wishes come true?
4. Distribute pebbles.
5. After they examine the pebbles, ask students to write a story about where they found the pebbles, what the pebbles looks like, and what happened. Share the stories.

EXTENSIONS

 VOCABULARY/SPELLING:

extraordinary   confused   perplexed
remarkable   ceased   puzzled
vanished   bewildered   scold

 **LIBRARY CONNECTIONS**

Caldecott Medal:

1. Divide the students into three groups.

- Group 1 locates other Caldecott books in the library.
- Group 2 looks up information on Randolph Caldecott. Use *A First Caldecott Collection* and *A Second Caldecott Collection*.
- Group 3 finds Caldecott's illustrations for Washington Irving's *Old Christmas* or William Cowper's *Mother Goose Rhymes*.

Hobbies and Collections:

1. Discuss hobbies and collections. Make a list of different hobbies and things people collect. Use the card catalog subject index to find information on these hobbies.
2. Use the dictionary and other library resources to research hobbies such as numismatics and philately.

Corpus of Work:

Collect and display other books by William Steig. Show *Doctor DeSoto*. Point out that this book won the Newbery Award. See if students can find Sylvester's family in Doctor DeSoto's waiting room.

❖ *Abel's Island*
❖ *Amos and Boris*
❖ *Brave Irene*
❖ *CDB*
❖ *Dominic*
❖ *Farmer Palmer's Wagon Ride*
❖ *Gorky Rises*
❖ *The Real Thief*
❖ *Roland the Minstrel Pig*
❖ *The Amazing Bone*
❖ *Solomon the Rusty Nail*
❖ *Spinky Sulkes*
❖ *Tiffky Doofky*
❖ *Yellow and Pink*
❖ *The Zabajaba Jungle*

 SCIENCE CONNECTIONS

1. Consult a book such as *The Herbal or General History of Plants* by John Gerard to research the herbs and spices alfalfa and sassafras. Students might write one interesting fact about each and explain why they found that fact interesting.
2. Make a list of other herb or spices the Duncans might take on a picnic.
3. Categorize the items the Duncans might take as either herbs, spices, grains, or grasses.

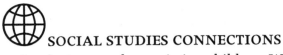SOCIAL STUDIES CONNECTIONS

Conduct research on missing children. Working in teams, students can interview the police. Check statistics on numbers of children missing according to grouped aged levels, such as five to seven years of age. Collect pictures of missing children. Find stories and first-person articles in magazines about missing children.

LANGUAGE ARTS CONNECTIONS

Personification:

Divide students into groups of three or four. Each group chooses an animal family. Each student within the group assumes the persona of one member of that animal family, such as the father, the baby, and they write a dialogue as if the animals were talking.

Letter writing:

Help students write to the local post office requesting information about the Benjamin Franklin Stamp Club.

ART CONNECTIONS

Make pomanders:

In medieval times, pomanders were worn to ward off disease and foul smells. Now they are usually hung in closets or put in drawers.

1. Mix ground spices, such as cinnamon, cloves, nutmeg, and ginger, in a bowl.
2. Push many whole cloves into an orange, lemon, lime, or apple so the spices will stick in and around the cloves.
3. Roll the clove-studded fruit in the ground spices, covering thoroughly.
4. Roll in a fixative such as orris root powder and set aside to dry.
5. Wrap the pomander in a fancy fabric and tie with a ribbon.

PUBLISHING

Plan a SYLVESTER PICNIC DAY. Place large pieces of colored butcher paper around the room as picnic blankets. Invite students to bring all their work from the Sylvester unit to share with their group. Distribute cups of fruit tea made from hibiscus, lemon grass, rose hips, orange peel, peppermint, and other things the Duncans might like. You might add oatmeal cookies.

12 Dr. JAC

Owl Moon

Jane Yolen

New York: Philomel Books, 1987. (Caldecott Winner)

Grade level: 3-8

Artifact: A "moon" cut from yellow paper

Summary: A father and daughter go owling in the winter under a full moon.

READING/WRITING CONNECTIONS

1. Write the word *owl* on the board or a chart. Invite students to make associations with *owl* while you write them down. Words like *wise* or comments such as "they can turn their heads all around" provide starting points for future research.
2. Introduce the book through its jacket. Students discuss the setting. Talk about the pictures on the title page and dedication pages. (Both the child and the owl are setting out; they meet within the pages of the story.) Read the two dedications. Ask the students how they feel about each.
3. Review metaphor and simile. Ask students to listen for such comparisons as you read.
4. Turn off the lights in the room and read the story in a whisper until you get to the line, "Time to go home," to capture the true experience and atmosphere of owling.
5. Distribute "moons." Ask students write an apt metaphor or simile on them.
6. Each student reads his or her "moon" aloud and then hangs it on a bulletin board you have covered with a deep blue (preferably shiny) paper.

EXTENSIONS

 VOCABULARY/SPELLING:

owling	crunched	crisp	bumped
quiet	pointy	icy	disappointed
furry	scarf	pumped	mittens
cloudy	echo	shadow	threading

 LIBRARY CONNECTIONS

Corpus of Work:

Check Sharron L. McElmeel's *Bookpeople: A First Album* for a partial list and *Books in Print* for a complete list of Jane Yolen's work. Gather as many of her books as possible to give students a sampling of the magnitude, complexity, and diversity of her work.

Owls:

1. Point out that this book won the Caldecott Medal. The illustrator is John Schoenherr. Students can appreciate its art, especially the page that depicts the owl. Invite comments.

2. Show students other owl books such as: Edward Lear's *The Owl and the Pussycat*. Point out Jan Brett and her illustrations. Compare and contrast it to Schoenherr's. Use also Howard Norman's *The Owl-Scatterer*. Point out wood engravings by Michael McCurdy as a type of artwork in this book. Compare and contrast this to the other two owl books.

3. Talk about how the art in a book adds to the enjoyment of the book as well as to its meaning.

Moons:

1. Share James Thurber's delightful story *Many Moons*, Phyllis Root's *Moon Tiger*, and Eric Carle's movable book *Papa, Please Get the Moon for Me*.

4. Discuss people's interest in the moon. Encourage students to speculate on that interest.

5. Share Byrd Baylor's *Moon Song*, which is the legend of the Moon giving birth to Coyote Child and evermore listening to the moon song of all coyotes. Share other moon myths.

Card or Computer Catalog:

Demonstrate how to use these catalogs to locate more information on the subject of owls or moons.

ENGLISH/LANGUAGE ARTS CONNECTIONS

Figurative Language:

1. Teach or review the metaphor and simile. Choose examples from the book. Talk about figurative language as one way to elaborate in writing.

2. Help students see (or hear) that "wise as an owl" has been used, is tired, is cliche; whereas, "Then the owl pumped its great wings and lifted off the branch like a shadow without sound." is a fresh, apt comparison that lets the reader see the owl in flight in a new and exciting way.

3. Use the owl's call as an example of onomatopoeia. Students find other examples in the book such as "crunching."

FOREIGN LANGUAGE CONNECTIONS

Read the poem "Lulu, Lulu, I've a Lilo" by Charlotte Pomerantz in Beatrice Schenk de Regniers' *Sing a Song of Popcorn*. This poem contains three Samoan words. Students translate those Samoan words into English and then rewrite the poem replacing the Samoan words with words from other languages.

 SCIENCE CONNECTIONS

1. Guide students, working in pairs, to use the encyclopedia and other reference books to gather general information about owls and specific information about the great horned owl. Then they design a unique way to share this information with the class, for example: posters, mobiles, murals, and so forth to share with the class.

2. Using science facts about owls, students working in small groups create an "Owl Trivia Game." Have them put their information on index cards and play their game with peers.

3. Let students use Peter Gill's *Birds* as a model book for their own owl books. They can find information to fit the categories of habitat, behavior, flight, shape, size, plumage, beaks, feet, eggs and nests, migration, even adding a glossary and index.

4. Share the information on the symbiosis of owls and blind snakes from "Strange Companions" in Lawrence E. Hillman's *Nature Puzzlers*.

5. Order owl pellets from a biological supply house. Discuss what owl pellets are and where they are found. Have students analyze them.

6. Return to the words suggested during the association time with the word *owl*. Students can choose one to research to uncover the scientific fact that it promotes.

 ART AND FILM CONNECTIONS

1. Show George Melies' short *A Trip to the Moon,* made in 1902. Melies' based his film on a Jules Verne story. (This film is in public domain and is easily found.) A historical note: the clip from this film of the rocket hitting the moon in the eye was shown on television during coverage of the first moon landing.

2. Invite students to fashion different owls out of clay. They mount and label each and provide an index card with pertinent information about that type of owl for display.

 PUBLISHING

Simulate Owling:

Turn the room lights off. Walk around in silence. Turn a flashlight on one or another of the clay owls, the owl books, or owl pictures on display. Students appreciate in silence. When the owling is over, say, "Time to go home." Students may then talk about the experience as they return to their places.

13

Dr. JAC

Wings

Jane Yolen

Harcourt Brace Jovanovich, 1991.

WINGS

JANE YOLEN

DENNIS NOLAN

Grade level: 3-12

Artifact: A feather

Summary: Imprisoned in Crete with his son Icarus, Daedalus fashions wings for their escape.

READING/WRITING CONNECTIONS

1. Talk about how people have always been fascinated by flight. Open the book so students see the front and back covers.
2. Invite speculations about the two main persons as well as those figures seen in the clouds.
3. Explain that because this book is based on a Greek myth, it is structured like a Greek drama, with an introduction, the story, a chorus, and an ending. Ask students to listen for these parts.
4. Read the introduction, chorus, and ending in a different tone than the story.
5. Distribute feathers. Invite students to follow Yolen's model and write a story using a feather or feathers as part of the plot. Share the stories.

EXTENSIONS

 VOCABULARY/SPELLING:

Daedalus	maze	labyrinth	Athens
Talos	exile	Crete	King Minos
Minotaur	cunning	Ariadne	Icarus
Theseus	pallets	nova	singe
Apollo	Sicily	King Cocalus	scabbed

 LIBRARY CONNECTIONS

Corpus of Work:

1. See *Bookpeople: A First Album* by Sharron L. McElmeel for information about Jane Yolen.

2. Share the information "About the Story" at the beginning of the book. Show students Homer's *The Illiad*. Read the poetic story from Ovid's *Metamorphoses*.

3. Use an etymological dictionary and the *Oxford English Dictionary* to trace the meaning of *hubris*. Discuss *hubris* in relation to the story.

4. Divide students into teams. Challenge the teams to find the names of other mythological creatures that are part one thing and part another, like the Minotaur, the sphinx, or harpies.

5. Let students choose one mythological creature from the list to research. Each team then shares its research with the other teams.

 ENGLISH/LANGUAGE ARTS CONNECTIONS

1. Read "Museé Des Beaux Arts" by Auden (in Abrams's *Norton Anthology)* and "Landscape With the Fall of Icarus," by William Carlos Williams. Discuss in relation to Brueghel's painting and the various mythologies.

2. Note the variations on the myth as found in Edith Hamilton's *Mythology* and *Bulfinch's Mythology* (compiled by Bryan Holme).

3. Read Warwick Hutton's *Theseus and the Minotaur*. Have students write a comparison/contrast paper using this version of the story and the one in *Wings*.

4. Read Elvira Woodruff's *The Wing Shop*. Ask students to write a comparison/contrast paper using this book and *Wings*.

5. Discuss the myth in relation to the Greek belief "Nothing in Excess."

6. Rewrite the myth from Icarus's point of view.

 ART CONNECTIONS

1. Study Pieter Brueghel the Elder's painting "The Fall of Icarus" which is in the Musee des Beaux Arts in Brussels, Belgium.

2. Divide students into four groups, each of which designs a labyrinth. When their designs are completed, have them draw it on butcher paper to be displayed in the room.

3. Create one of the sixteen flying machines, using the models of Dennis Hommel from *Sixteen Flying Machines*.

 SCIENCE CONNECTIONS

1. Construct a time line on the history of flight. Use "Landmarks in Aviation History"

in Jerry D. Flack's *Inventing, Inventions, and Inventors: A Teaching Resource Book* as a model.

2. Research heavier-than-air-flight. Then test the research by making and flying a kite.

3. Ask students to research the axe, bevel, and awl and write an article on each implement, using *Simple Machines* by Rae Bains as their model.

4. Conduct the experiment with the ant and the seashell, described on the last page of the book.

5. Research the birds mentioned in the book: gulls, gannets, petrels, cormorants, pelicans, shearwaters, grebes. Find one interesting fact about each bird.

6. Discuss Daedalus as a scientist. Should a scientist consider the social, political, and economic effects of his or her invention? Should a scientist forego inventing something detrimental to personkind? Should scientists create for dictators?

7. Research Leonardo da Vinci's ideas for flying machines.

 SOCIAL STUDIES CONNECTIONS

Map Study:

1. Locate Athens, Greece. Write out its latitude and longitude.
2. Locate the island of Crete. Write out its latitude and longitude.
3. Locate the isle of Sicily and determine its latitude and longitude.

Political Science:

Hold a mock trial. Put Daedalus on trial for the murder of Icarus. Divide students into defense attorneys and prosecutors. Each lawyer will write a brief in which the evidence is used to convince the jury that Daedalus is guilty or innocent. The class will act as the jury.

 MATHEMATICS CONNECTIONS

1. Have students estimate the distance between Athens and Crete. Then, using and atlas and its key, they check the accuracy of their estimates.

2. After estimating the distance between Crete and Sicily, students can use the atlas and its key to check the accuracy of their estimates.

 DRAMA CONNECTIONS

Students perform the play *Daedalus*. This play, in two acts for eight characters, can be found in Josephine Davidson's *Teaching and Dramatizing Greek Myths*.

PUBLISHING

Create a display, FACTS AND MYTHS ABOUT FLYING, using books and the writing and research of students.

14

Dr. JAC

The Magic Fan

Keith Baker

Harcourt Brace Jovanovich, 1989

Grade level: 3-6

Artifact: A paper fan

Summary: Yoshi makes decisions based on what he sees in a fan until he discovers the *magic* was in himself not in the fan.

READING/WRITING CONNECTIONS

1. Hold a closed accordion-style fan, preferably one with a picture on it. Open it slowly in front of the students. Allow them to discover and discuss its picture.
2. Open the book so that the students see the front and back jacket. Encourage them to discover the picture on the fan. Using the picture, students speculate on the setting of this book (Japan).
3. Tell the students that there is something special about the way this book works: its form is like a fan because its meaning is about a fan. Talk about why they think the author would choose a fan as a symbol for his story. How is a story like a fan? How is a discovery like a fan?
4. After reading the story, distribute unlined paper so students may write about a time when they discovered something they could do well. On the other side, they illustrate that time.
5. Show students how to make their papers into fans by folding them accordion-style.
6. Divide students into groups of three to share their fans.

EXTENSIONS

 VOCABULARY/SPELLING:

hull	stitched	horizon	enormous
trembled	earthquake	twisted	thrashed
Namazu	monstrous	Yoshi	Tsunami

LIBRARY CONNECTIONS

1. Tell students this book won the *School Library Journal* Best Book award. Talk about what they think makes this an award-winning book.
2. Share other books about Japan:
   ❖ *The Crane Wife,* retold by Sumiko Yagawa (translated by Katherine Paterson)
   ❖ *The Bicycle Man* by Allen Say
   ❖ *The Badger and the Magic Fan* adapted by Tony Johnston
   ❖ *The Tale of the Mandarin Ducks* by Katherine Paterson
   ❖ *The Boy of the Three-Year Nap* by Dianne Snyder

 ENGLISH/LANGUAGE ARTS CONNECTIONS

Writing for different purposes and modes:

1. Students write a "how to" paper explaining how to make a paper fan.
2. Students write a comparison/contrast paper on Japan then and now.
3. Students write an informative paper about Japan.

Writing Haiku and Tanka Poems:

Teach Haiku and Tanka poetry forms. Haiku uses three lines of seven, five, and seven syllables.

Tanka uses five lines of seven, five, seven, five, and five syllables.

 SOCIAL STUDIES CONNECTIONS

1. Help students construct a dimensional map of Japan using papier-mâché or baker's clay. (See Dr. JAC 2).
2. Ask students to research village life in Japan and compare it to small-town life in the United States.
3. Through research on development of bridges, students may:
   • Describe early bridges (rope walkways, arched brick or stone structures).
   • Tell how the advent of steel aided the construction of bridges.
   • Write about why movable bridges are important.
   • Find out what a military bridge is and how it differs from a regular bridge.
   • Research famous bridges such as the Brooklyn Bridge, the Golden Gate Bridge, or the Verrazano-Narrows Bridge.
   • If there is a bridge in your area, investigate its origin, structure, purpose.

SCIENCE CONNECTIONS

1. Bend a plastic ruler until it breaks. After that introduction, compare the ruler to the earth's crust. Use that as an object lesson to begin the study of earthquakes. See Zuza Vrbova's *Volcanoes and Earthquakes* for interesting information on "Forecasting Earthquakes."

2. Create rainbows by hanging prisms in windows. Ask students to research why they create rainbows.

3. Experiment with rainbows. Place water in a shallow, square pan. Set a mirror at a slight angle at one end of the pan. Shine a flashlight at a 30-degree angle at the mirror through the water. A rainbow with appear above the mirror. List the colors that can be seen.

ART CONNECTIONS

Celebrate a Japanese village cherry blossom festival by making cherry blossom place mats.

- Divide students into groups of 4 or 5. Distribute white paper the size of a standard place mat and a drinking straw to each student.
- Give each group a small cup of pink or red watercolor paint.
- Put a drop of india ink on each paper. Let students create tree and branch configurations by blowing through the straw, held diagonally to the paper. This will not work if the straw is at a right angle to the paper.
- When the ink is dry, students put their little finger in the pink or red paint and dot the trees and branches to make cherry blossoms.
- They then choose an area of the paper on which to write their haiku or tanka.
- Laminate the papers to use as display and later send home to be used as place mats.

PUBLISHING

Conduct a JAPANESE TEA CELEBRATION. Research favorite Japanese teas. If Japanese teas are unavailable, substitute any tea.

Your Own Best Secret Place

Byrd Baylor and Peter Parnall

Charles Scribner's Sons, 1979

Grade level: All levels

Artifact: A brown paper bag

Summary: A young girl discovers that a hollow of a tree is a secret place. She respects its privacy and extends that respect to the secret places of others.

READING/WRITING CONNECTIONS

1. Hold a red coffee can. When you get to the part in the story where the girl looks into the red coffee can, invite speculation about its contents.
2. Take out each item: a pencil stub, a knife with two blades, a burned-down candle, a feather, and a drawing.
3. Continue reading to the part where the girl wonders why William Cottonwood left those items. Again invite speculation.
4. After completing the book, take the students through a memory inventory. Ask them to close their eyes as you suggest images of a place they considered secret as a child. Suggest images that would trigger sights, smells, sounds, tastes, and feelings associated with that place. Discuss what they remembered.
5. Distribute the brown bags. Invite students to write about their secret place on the paper bags; they may also tear or cut the bags to create a simulation of their secret place.
6. Share in small groups.

EXTENSIONS

 VOCABULARY/SPELLING:

chile	thickets	swoop	shafts
hollow	gully	canyon	dune

 **LIBRARY CONNECTIONS**

Corpus of Work:

1. Share other books that have a "secret" in them such as
    ❖Joan Lowery Nixon's *Secret, Silent Screams*
    ❖Catherine Brighton's *Five Secrets in a Box*
    ❖Marilee Heyer's *The Forbidden Door*
    ❖Florence Parry Heide & Judith Heide Gilliland's *The Day of Ahmed's Secret.*

2. Students tell about other "secret" books they know.

 ENGLISH/LANGUAGE ARTS CONNECTIONS

Proper Nouns:

1. Brainstorm the proper nouns students remember from the book. Write these on the board, using this as a time to reteach why each begins with a capital letter.

2. Reinforce the difference of common and proper nouns by writing *cottonwood trees* and *William Cottonwood* and talking about that difference.

Writing Notes:

Examine the notes left by William Cottonwood. Discuss them. Elicit from the students their criteria for a good note. Write a note to someone. Share notes. Talk about their clarity, brevity, and purpose.

"Secret" Words:

Have students, working in pairs, use their library information skills to formulate lists of compound words, terms, labels, products and so forth that have the the word *secret* in them. For example: secret police, Secret™ deodorant, secretion.

"Secrets":

Read "Secrets" by Judith Viorst in *If I Were in Charge of the World and Other Worries*. Play the "Gossip Game." Discuss how and why the story changes from beginning to end. How does that affect anything "secret"?

 SOCIAL STUDIES CONNECTIONS

1. Study the topography of the areas mentioned in the book:
    • a river valley in New Mexico
    • a sandy gully in Texas
    • hay field in Montana
    • sand dune in Arizona
    • pear orchard in Virginia

2. Study the similarities and differences in the commerce and cultures of these areas.

SCIENCE CONNECTIONS

1. List all the birds and animals Baylor mentions in her book:

   pinon jays   small owls   beavers   badgers
   fox   rabbits   mice

2. Working in teams of three, research each of these birds and animals. Find out about their habitats. Each team decides upon one interesting fact about each animal and shares its choices of facts with other teams.

 ART CONNECTIONS

1. Position students in various places in the room—on the floor, in the corners, facing interesting but unusual ways.

2. Give each student an index card with a small hole cut out of it.

3. As students look through the holes, they draw what they see, just as William Cottonwood must have drawn what he saw when looking out his tree hollow.

 PUBLISHING

Have students bring in a coffee can, oatmeal box, or other container into which they have placed several special but shareable items, their drawing, and something they have written. On Secret Place Day, share these in small groups.

16

A Medieval Feast

Aliki

New York: Harper & Row, 1983

Grade level: 3-12

Artifact: A piece of paper that has been aged by searing and burning its edges with a candle or by rubbing it with brown water color

Summary: The king and queen visit an English manor house where elaborate preparations have been made for a feast during their visit.

READING/WRITING CONNECTIONS

1. Tell students as you read they are to pretend they will be the royal guests, the recipients of all the preparations described in the book.
2. Read the two dedication pages, one to the Medieval artists who inspired the illustrations in the book and one personal.
3. As you read the first page, play any musical recording by the composer William Byrd.
4. Linger over the pages so students have time to notice all the details.
5. Distribute a piece of the *aged paper* (paper soaked in tea) to each student.
6. Have students write journal entries on the *aged paper* as if they were the king or queen writing in their journals after the feast. Ask them to describe the feast in general and then describe in detail the part they liked best. Encourage them to elaborate, to be creative, and to extend what they heard and saw in the book. For example, the book mentions jugglers but does not describe them.
7. Share journal entries. Then collate them into a book with a leather-like or wooden cover and display it.

EXTENSIONS

destination	manor	squires	serfs	estate
suite	marzipan	provisions	poaching	boar
capon	tapestries	panter	ewerer	crest

LIBRARY CONNECTIONS

Corpus of Work:

See Sharron L. McElmeel's *Bookpeople: A First Album* for more information on Aliki.

Medieval Life:

Help students explore the library for information on festivals, courts and courtiers, state visits, and medieval life.

Nursery Rhymes:

Review the nursery rhymes that contain references to this period of history. For example, "Sing A Song of Sixpence" and "The King Was in His Counting House" can be found in Colgin's *One Potato, Two Potato, Three Potato, Four*

Additional books:

Share Joe Lasker's *Merry Ever After: The Story of Two Medieval Weddings* and *A Tournament of Knights* and Mitsumasa Anno's *Anno's Medieval World*.

 ENGLISH/LANGUAGE ARTS/ ART CONNECTIONS

Heraldry:

1. Read the book by Dana Fradon *Harold the Herald: A Book About Heraldry* as an elaboration of the reference to the King's crest, or use Jonathan Hunt's *Illuminations*. In the back of *Illuminations,* Hunt talks about the fun he had creating his shield for the coat of arms in the book. He also suggests his favorite King Arthur books and provides an informative bibliography.

2. Help students design shields with their own crest. Develop these crests by using the suggestions in Edward Wilson's article "Shielding the Basic Student."
   - Draw a shape and section it into four quarters and a center section.
   - Draw (or cut out pictures) for all five sections to represent:
     - ❖ something about their lives (plot);
     - ❖ where they have lived or where they live now (setting);
     - ❖ some people in their lives (characters);
     - ❖ their favorite saying, one that applies to their lives (theme);
     - ❖ (the center) their symbol (symbolism).
     - ❖ share these, explaining the reasons for their choices.

3. Shields can be displayed in the room and referred to when studying literature with these elements to provide a concrete point of reference.

SCIENCE CONNECTIONS

1. Working in groups of four, students research the animals, birds, fish shown in the book. They write the name of an animal, bird or fish on the front of an index card and write one interesting fact on the back. These can be used to play "Medieval Trivial Pursuit."

2. Working in groups of four, students research the fruits, vegetables, herbs, and flowers shown in the book. They may bring in examples or share interesting facts about them.

SOCIAL STUDIES CONNECTIONS

1. Read Helldorfer's *The Mapmaker's Daughter*. Students can pretend they are Suchen and they must make a map for the king from his palace to Camdenton Manor.

2. Research medieval manor houses. Make a series of dioramas to represent the manor: royal suite, the tented yard, the forest, the rivers and creeks, the garden, the mills and ovens, the wine presses and vineyard, the kitchen, and the great feasting hall.

3. Use John S. Goodall's wordless *The Story of a Main Street* to show the evolution of a street from medieval times to the present. Students can create their own versions of the evolution of foods, clothing, houses, customs, territory using the information they find in their research.

π MATHEMATICS CONNECTIONS

1. Create a key to the map. Measure the distance from the palace to Camdenton. Estimate the number of days it would take to travel that distance during medieval times.

2. Calculate the number of hours the people feasted if they began as the book says "at half past ten in the morning" and "ate until dark."

PUBLISHING

Refer to Jan Irving's *Fanfares: Programs for Classrooms and Libraries* for ideas to plan and celebrate a classroom MEDIEVAL FEAST. Designate jesters, jugglers, and minstrels.

17

Dr. JAC

The Keeping Quilt

Patricia Polacco

New York:Simon & Schuster, 1988

Grade level: All levels

Artifact:A seven-inch square of material in different patterns

Summary:A quilt passed through four generations remains as a testimony of a Russian Jewish family's love and faith.

READING/WRITING CONNECTIONS

1. Bring or have a student bring a quilt to begin this lesson. Talk about the way quilts are made, who makes them, and why.
2. Introduce the book by opening the book so the full jacket can be seen. Discuss.
3. Examine the title and copyright pages. Invite speculation about who these people might be and why the Statue of Liberty is pictured.
4. After reading the book, students choose their square of material from the selection offered.
5. Students cut out animals, flowers, or designs from their material. Each student pastes his or her design on a piece of construction paper and writes: its description (including color, size, pattern) and why it is important. Share.

EXTENSIONS

 VOCABULARY/SPELLING:

artificial	babushka	Vladimir	Havalah
Natasha	Russia	Sabbath	challah
Sasha	handkerchief	huppa	bouquet
kulich	candied	Amazon	Enzo-Mario

LIBRARY CONNECTIONS

Corpus of work:

Share

❖ *Thunder Cake*

❖ *Babushka's Doll*

❖ *Just Plain and Fancy*

❖ *Boatride with Lillian Two-Blossom*

❖ *Rechenka's Eggs*

❖ *Meteor*

all by Patricia Polacco.

Additional Quilt books:

Display other quilt books, perhaps on a quilt:

❖ Eleanor Coerr's *The Josefina Story Quilt*, set in 1850, involves a pet hen;

❖ Natalie Kinsey-Warnock's *The Canada Geese Quilt*, set in the 1940's, tells how ten-year old Ariel makes a special quilt;

❖ Ann Whitford Paul's *Eight Hands Round: A Patchwork Alphabet* book combines the letters of the alphabet with names of quilt designs;

❖ David McKee's *Elmer* tells the story of a patchwork elephant;

❖ Tony Johnston and Tomie dePaola's *The Quilt Story* recounts how a pioneer woman makes a quilt to comfort her little girl and how that quilt later comforts another little girl;

❖ Ann Jonas' *The Quilt* tells how a quilt can bring memories and adventures;

❖ Mary Whittington's *The Patchwork Lady* prepares her patchwork house for her birthday party;

❖ Valerie Flournoy's *The Patchwork Quilt* becomes the vehicle through which a grandmother tells the story of the family;

❖ Faith Ringgold's *Tar Beach* is a story based on the author's quilt painting.

 SOCIAL STUDIES CONNECTIONS

1. Use this book as a springboard into work on immigrations to America's New York Harbor from 1892 to 1924. Extend that lesson to include Ellis Island, the place where immigrants stayed until they were given their "landing cards." Students can conduct research using Lydia Anderson's *Immigration* and Beatrice Siegel's *Sam Ellis's Island*. Conclude the work with Riki Levinson's *Watch the Stars Come Out*, which tells the story of coming to America by boat and spotting the Statue of Liberty.

2. Make maps that trace the trips of people coming from Poland, Russia, and other countries to America.

3. Research the Alien and Sedition Acts; Chinese Exclusion Act; Immigration

Restriction League; Russian Revolution; Statue of Liberty National Monument.

 MATHEMATICS CONNECTIONS

Estimate the distance and time it would take people from departure to destination to get from various countries to America. Calculate weather and time of year as variables.

 MUSIC CONNECTIONS

Research and sing folk songs of the immigrating peoples.

 ENGLISH/LANGUAGE ARTS CONNECTIONS

1. Students pick another square of material.
2. Students fold an eight-page book. (See Dr. JAC 3)
3. In their books they write the story of a family treasure, something that has been passed down through the generations, that has been given from one family member to another, or that they might give. Staple the squares of material onto a bulletin board. After sharing, each student staples a book onto a square as if on a large quilt that reflects the class's collective effort. This is particularly good for Parents' Nights or School Open Houses.

 ART CONNECTIONS

Challenge students to create an original design for a patchwork quilt. Encourage students to look with new eyes at the things around them as people did in the past when they captured the design of tools, toys, animals, plants, stars, events, or a people.

 PUBLISHING

Celebrate with a QUILTING PARTY. Invite students to bring in quilts from home to display. Gather the students in a circle. Each can share a quilt design. Serve lemonade and ginger cookies.

*Knots on a
Counting Rope*

Bill Martin, Jr. and
John Archambault

Henry Holt & Co.,
1987

Grade level: 3-12

Artifact: A fifteen-inch piece of heavy twine

Summary: Grandfather and Boy-Strength-of-Blue-Horses retell stories that center around the boy's life.

READING/WRITING CONNECTIONS

1. Show students the title page. Invite predictions about the story.
2. Read the story in two voices or read the story with a student.
3. Give each student their artifacts. Explain that they are to keep their ropes for the entire unit. Each time they read aloud something they have written, they tie a knot on their counting ropes.
4. Give students time to write about a time they crossed "dark mountains."
5. Using "dark mountains" writings, have students in groups of three follow steps:
   • The writer reads. Pauses. Reads again.
   • Listeners listen. Upon the second reading, they jot down what they like and what they want to know more about, and they *say* these things *back* to the writer.
6. Each writer gets to tie two knots on his or her counting rope.

EXTENSIONS

 VOCABULARY/SPELLING:

afraid	bobcat	heart-pounding	frail
shallow	breath	galloping	strength
ceremony	curtain	rainbow	foal
reins	tribal	courage	mountains

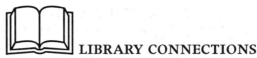 LIBRARY CONNECTIONS

Additional books:

1. Use *Keepers of the Earth: Native American Stories and Environmental Activities for Children* by Michael J. Caduto and Joseph Bruchac with its accompanying teacher's guide. This set is a rich resource on everything from "Science and Indian Myths" to "The Origin of Death."

2. Show students where they can find more information on American Indians in the library.

3. Share other books that have American Indian legends or myths. For example:

   ❖ Tomie dePaola's *The Legend of the Indian Paintbrush,* and *The Legend of the Bluebonnet*

   ❖ Gerald McDermott's *Arrow to the Sun*

   ❖ Sheila MacGill-Callahan's *And Still the Turtle Watched*

   ❖ Jane Yolen's *Sky Dogs*

   ❖ *The Night the White Deer Died* by Gary Paulsen (for older students).

4. Expose students to American Indian mythologies. Ron Smith's *Mythologies of the World: A Guide to Sources* is an excellent resource for hundreds of books dealing with this topic.

 SOCIAL STUDIES/ 𝛑 MATHEMATICS CONNECTIONS

Working in groups of three or four students:

• Draw a map or create a three-dimensional map of the trails for the race, using the description in the book.

• Create a key that conveys the scale of miles.

• Compute the distance Boy-Strength-of-Blue-Horses had to travel for the race.

• Estimate the time it would have taken him to run the race on Rainbow.

 ART CONNECTIONS

1. Create murals of some aspect of the story. For example, they may design a rainbow.

2. Model sculptures out of clay about some aspect of the story. For example, they may create a blue horse.

 MUSIC/ ★ DRAMA CONNECTIONS

1. Using Paul Fleischman's *I Am Phoenix: Poems for Two Voices* as their model, students working in groups, create poems for two such as:

• "I Am Blue Horses." Encourage students to read about legends related to blue and horses.

- "I Am Rainbow." Encourage them to research rainbow colors.

2. Boy-Strength-of-Blue-Horses discovers blue. Prepare a dramatic reading of his discovery.

3. Prepare a dramatic reading of "Windy Nights" by Robert Louis Stevenson (found in Beatrice Schenk de Regniers' *Sing a Song of Popcorn*. Emphasize the "gallop."

4. Play "Listen to the Horses" in *The Raffi Singable Songs Collection*. Students join in the singing as they learn the song.

ENGLISH/LANGUAGE ARTS CONNECTIONS

Naming:

1. Investigate the power and symbolism of names:
Students conduct an "I-Search" about their own first name, following the concept from Ken Macrorie's *The I-Search Paper*. They may interview relatives to uncover the source of their name. (If students don't live with family, they can research the name they would like to have.) When writing about their findings, they should include the name, its source (why they were given this name), and what it means.

2. Help students research the origins of their favorite names or the names of their favorite characters in literature. Names are often significant to the story.

Compound words:

Teach compound words by pulling them from the story and writing them on the board or chart.

- Brainstorm literal definitions of those words. For example, students might define grandfather literally as a *big father* or a *big daddy*.
- Check definitions against the dictionary.
- Add to the class' *Word Bank*.

Poetic devices:

Use the rich figurative language in this book to teach such poetic devices as personification, symbolism, alliteration, consonance, dramatic dialogue, analogy, imagery, simile, metaphor, repetition, and rhythm.

PUBLISHING

Have a COUNTING OF THE KNOTS. At the conclusion of the unit, students count their knots, write the number on a card, and hang the knots and card on the bulletin board or designated place. Celebrate by sitting in a circle and talking about what was learned during this unit.

19

The Goat in the Rug

Geraldine (as told to Charles L. Blood and Martin Link)

Macmillan Publishing Company, 1976

Grade level: 5-7

Artifact: Several strands of red, brown, black, and white yarn knotted as a set

Summary: Geraldine the goat tells how her Navajo friend, Glenmae, makes a rug. She describes each step from the hair cutting to the rug weaving.

READING/WRITING CONNECTIONS

1. Take one yarn set and braid it in front of the students. Explain that braiding is one way to work the yarn. Ask them if they know other ways.
2. Talk about weaving. Then tell them the book you are about to read is a how-to book because it tells how to make a rug.
3. Show the book. Talk about the author. Discuss point of view.
4. Invite predictions about who the other person pictured on the cover might be.
5. As you read, point out the Navajo designs on each picture.
6. Distribute the sets of yarn strands and let students braid their yarn.
7. Have them write directions on how to braid yarn.
8. Have them undo their yarn braids, get with a partner, and exchange directions.
9. Have them braid their yarn again following their partner's directions.
10. Discuss what happened. Discuss the importance of accuracy in writing directions.

EXTENSIONS

 VOCABULARY/SPELLING:

Geraldine	Window Rock	Navajo	Glenmae
Glee Nasbah	warrior	weaver	scissors
mohair	ticklish	yucca	soapy
lather	carding combs	burrs	fibers
spindle	dye	dyeing	delicious
wrapping	loom	design	duplicated

 **LIBRARY CONNECTIONS**

1. Share other how-to books:

❖Tomie dePaola's *The Popcorn Book* tells how to make popcorn, and *The Quicksand Book* tells how to make quicksand. Both give recipes.

❖Gail Gibbons's *How a House is Built* tells how a house is made and her *The Pottery Place* tells how a pot is made.

2. Direct students to areas in the library where they can find more information on the Navajo Nation at Window Rock, Arizona.

3. Help students locate information on weaving.

4. Share another Navajo story about weaving:

❖Miska Miles' *Annie and the Old One*. In this poignant story Annie undid her grandmother's weaving so that the old one would not die.

SCIENCE/ π MATHEMATICS CONNECTIONS

Dyeing:

1. Experiment with dyeing eggs, paper, and pieces of cloth. Fill cups with hot water and cold water. Add food coloring or dye from store-bought packets. Dip each item. Calculate the amount of time it takes to dye to the desired color in the hot water and in the cold water. Draw conclusions.

2. Graph the number of dips needed to achieve the desired color.

3. Make dyes. Using the items pictured on the endpapers of the book, try making dyes from walnuts, juniper berries, dock, wild onion, rabbit brush, cliff rose, or sumac. Contact The American Herb Association, P.O. 353, Rescue, CA. 95672 for sources for these items.

4. Locate Rita J. Adrosko's *Natural Dyes and Home Dyeing* as a source book.

Identifying plants/research:

Bring in walnuts, juniper berries, dock, wild onion, rabbit brush, cliff rose, sumac, pinyon pine, yucca.

• Students mount each specimen and label it.

• They research some interesting information about each.

• They write that information next to each mounted item.

SOCIAL STUDIES/ π MATHEMATICS CONNECTIONS

The Navajo Nation:

1. Research information about the Navajo Indians, their nation, and their history.

2. Write for a copies of the *Navajo Tribal Newspaper*, the largest in the United States.

3. Write for information about the Navajo Community College, the first Native-

American-operated college.

4. Find out information about Navajo weaving and rugs. Hypothesize why they are so prized.

Map study:

1. Find Window Rock, Arizona on a map. Calculate the extent of the Navajo Nation's 16 million acres which reach from Arizona into New Mexico and Utah.

2. Plot a route from where you are to Window Rock. Calculate the distance using the map's legend. Calculate the time it would take by car, by plane, by train, by covered wagon, and by horse.

 ENGLISH/LANGUAGE ARTS CONNECTIONS

Sequence Word Review:

1. Review sequence words. Remind students that authors use these words so that readers understand the time order of story events.

2. Explain that you will reread the book. Every time students hear a sequence word, they are to raise their hands.

3. Write a how-to book.

 ART CONNECTIONS

1. Ask students to design and make the covers for their books. Talk about the appropriateness of the covers and how the covers should reflect in some way the contents of the book.

2. Have students also design and write a dedication page and an "About the Author" page.

 PUBLISHING

Display all the how-to books made by the students. Call display How-To!

The Empty Pot

Demi

Henry Holt and Company, 1990

THE EMPTY POT

DEMI

Grade level: Pre-K-2

Artifact: A one to two inch clay pot

Summary: Ping, who cannot grow a flower from the seed given him by the Emperor, is rewarded for doing his best and for being honest.

READING/WRITING CONNECTIONS

The Best of Story Books
61

1. Show the students how the pictures in the book are the same shape as the round pot.
2. Ask them to describe what the students are doing on the title page.
3. Read the dedication. Ask students if they can guess by the pictures where this story takes place (China).
4. Read the story. Give ample time for the students to look at the pictures.
5. When you get to the two-page spread of the Emperor on one page and Ping on the other, ask students about feelings: theirs, Ping's, the Emperor's. Ask if the picture helps them feel. Talk about that.
6. After the reading, talk about Ping and why he was rewarded. Discuss honesty.
7. Distribute the tiny pots. Students write their names on the pots with indelible markers. They may also decorate the pots. Distribute large circular pieces of paper to students. Ask the students to draw pictures of their pots in the circles and write or draw what they would like to grow in their pots. Share.

EXTENSIONS

 VOCABULARY/SPELLING:

China	Ping	kingdom	perfume
Emperor	tended	successor	throne
proclamation	issued	palace	succeed
excitement	beautiful	flowerpot	sprout
blossom	transferred	soil	eagerly

| ashamed | clever | overhead | frowning |
| punished | exclaimed | cooked | impossible |

LIBRARY CONNECTIONS

Corpus of work:

1. Share with students *Demi's Opposites: An Animal Game Book.* Use this to review numbers and animals and to teach or reteach the concept of opposite. Use it also to teach the concepts of empty and full. Be certain to show the dedication page. Here Demi shows his two-year-old nephew's drawing of a bird.
2. Share *Demi's Reflections.* Encourage them to look into the mirror and tell stories about what they see there.
3. Share *Chingis Khan,* the story of the Mongol leader, which begins when he was a little boy.

Other Chinese Folktales:

1. Margaret Mahy's *The Seven Chinese Brothers,* although fictional, is based on the Emperor Ch'in Shih Huang, who is credited with unifying China and planning the Great Wall. This story is also one in which justice is served.
2. Thomas Handforth's *Mei Li* (a Caldecott winner) tells a delightful story of a little girl who is curious and adventuresome.
3. Robert D. San Souci's *The Enchanted Tapestry* describes how Li Ju tries to reclaim his mother's tapestry from the fairies of Sun Mountain.

SCIENCE CONNECTIONS

1. Talk about seeds and how they grow. Talk about why cooked seeds such as those the Emperor gave Ping and the other children could not grow. Talk about what seeds need to help them grow.
2. Read Eric Carle's *The Tiny Seed* (optional).
3. Bring in different kinds of seeds: millet, sunflower seeds, apple seeds, a peach or pear pit, cherry pits, a variety of flower seeds, several different kinds of nuts. Talk about them.
4. On a table or counter, arrange some soil, some birdseed, and some water. Have each student plant some of the birdseed in his or her pot.
5. Display where the pots get sun.
6. Students record in round books (see Art Connections) the progress of their seeds from planting to sprouting.

ART CONNECTIONS

To make round books:

1. Students trace a 12-inch circle onto four pieces of paper.
2. Cut out the four circles and fold them in half.
3. Sew the four circles together on the fold with dental floss (or an adult can stitch four circles sets together on a sewing machine.) Pages will open in half circles.
5. Spatter-paint the covers. Glue on pieces of colorful tissue in flower patterns.

 MATHEMATICS CONNECTIONS

Reinforce the concept of round by inviting the students to find round objects in the room and naming them. Put the names of the round objects on the board. Students may enter these in their round books.

PUBLISHING

Display students' round books along with their pots. Make a bulletin board that says OUR POTS AND OUR BOOKS ARE FULL! Open *Demi's Opposites* to the "empty/full" page. Add other appropriate books.

21 *Harry and the Terrible Whatzit*

Dick Gackenbach

Clarion Books, 1977

Grade level: 1-3

Artifact: A miniature broom made from match sticks or toothpicks and straw

Summary: Harry goes down the cellar where he confronts and overcomes a terrible Whatzit and his own fear.

READING/WRITING CONNECTIONS

1. Begin with a brief story about hearing sounds one night while you were in bed. (You might even tap the board or chair.) Ask students if they ever hear sounds when they are in bed. Discuss

2. Continue by saying that after you heard the sounds, you threw aside the drapes and saw a terrible Whatzit! When they ask, "What's a Whatzit?" introduce the book.

3. After reading, ask students to talk about what makes them afraid. Accept all responses: the dark, the dentist, scary television shows, and so forth.

4. Make the tiny brooms by taping some straw on the ends of a match stick or toothpick. Then tape the brooms to a piece of paper.

5. Students imagine and write about holding the broom as they confront their fear. Share.

EXTENSIONS

 VOCABULARY/SPELLING:

terrible	cellar	pickles	gloomy
furnace	Whatzit	runt	swat
twisted	shrank	peanut	disappeared
washer	boxes	wood bin	glasses

LIBRARY CONNECTIONS

Corpus of work:

1. Share other works of the author:
   - ❖ *A Bag Full of Pups*
   - ❖ *Binky Gets a Car*
   - ❖ *Claude and Pepper*
   - ❖ *Dog for a Day*
   - ❖ *Harvey the Foolish Pig*
   - ❖ *Hurray for Hattie Rabbit*
   - ❖ *Poppy the Panda*
   - ❖ *With Love From Gran*

2. See Sharron L. McElmeel's *Bookpeople: A First Album* for biographical information about the author.

   Other "Monster" Books:
   - ❖ Share Teddy Slater's *Molly's Monsters*
   - ❖ Maurice Sendak's *Where the Wild Things Are*
   - ❖ Mercer Mayer's *There's Something In My Attic*, and *There's a Nightmare In My Closet*
   - ❖ Brinton Turkle's *Do Not Open*.

   "Monster" Poetry:
   Jack Prelutsky's "Something Big Has Been Here" in the book by the same title and Walter de la Mare's "Someone" in de Regnier's collection *Sing a Song of Popcorn*.

 **ART/ MUSIC CONNECTIONS**

1. Distribute 12-inch by 18-inch pieces of paper. Following your model, students fold their papers into thirds.

2. On the board, draw a rectangle and indicate the folds with dotted lines.

3. Ask students to imagine a terrible Whatzit. Then ask about its heads: their number, shape, size, color, and face parts.

4. Holding the paper vertically, students draw their Whatzit's heads in the top panel of the paper as you draw yours on the board (use colored chalk).

5. At your signal, the students walk around with their drawings, looking at each other's and singing "Who's Afraid of the Big Bag Whatzit?" and ending each verse with "Not me."

6. When you say, "Stop!" the students freeze and exchange papers with a nearby student. Then they return to their seats.

7. Follow the same procedure for the body in the middle panel.

8. Follow the same procedure for the legs and tail in the bottom panel. Then students find their Whatzits by looking for the head they drew.

MATHEMATICS CONNECTIONS

Bring in an assortment of things that have three parts, such as: a boiled egg—yolk, white, shell; an apple—seeds, pulp, skin; a peanut butter and jelly sandwich—peanut butter, jelly, bread; pencil—lead, wood, eraser; box of cereal—box, waxed paper inside, cereal; a story—beginning, middle, end. Talk about these. Have students look around the room and identify other things that have three parts.

SCIENCE CONNECTIONS

Insects' Three Body Parts:

1. Insects have three main body parts: a head, a thorax, and an abdomen. Distribute plastic insects or pictures of insects. Students identify the three body parts.
2. Students draw an insect. They name it and label its three body parts.

ENGLISH/LANGUAGE ARTS CONNECTIONS

Hyphens in Compound Words:

1. List the compound hyphenated words from the story:
   double-headed
   three-clawed
   six-toed
   long-horned
2. Teach that most of the time when two closely-related words describe a naming word (adjectives), those words are joined with a hyphen to help the reader see that they all go together. For example: six-toed Whatzit.

Paragraphing:

1. Invite students to speculate on how they can tell where one part of the Whatzit ends and another begins (by the folds).
2. Show them several books. Explain that when authors want to go to another part they also do something to signal the reader.
3. Invite students to examine the writing in the books. Eventually they will tell you some variation of "It's dented in."
4. Hold a soda can. Dent in it with your thumb.
5. Draw a rectangle on the board to match students' papers. Show how to push the thumb in from the margin "about a thumb's worth" to make a paragraph dent.
6. Tell students that is how to begin a paragraph.

Descriptive writing:

Talk about how books have pictures and words to help the reader understand the meaning. Tell them that as authors they can match their pictures with words. They write: *(THEIR NAME) and the Terrible Whatzit* as the title of the paper. They describe their Whatzit, ("denting in") each time they begin a new part of the description.

 PUBLISHING

An Author's Chair Share:

Pick the first author to sit in the chair and share. That author picks someone to hold the Whatzit's picture during the reading. After each author reads, the author may pick two or three students to tell what they liked. They must be specific. For example: I liked the way you said your Whatzit had a head shaped like a taco." This follow-up is a good way to hone listening skills. The author then picks the next author. Display the Whatzits and their descriptions around the room or in the hall.

Earrings!

Judith Viorst

New York: Atheneum, 1990

Grade level: 7-11

Artifact: An earring or inexpensive gold rings available as souvenirs for weddings and showers.

Summary: A young girl tries to persuade her parents to let her have her ears pierced.

READING/WRITING CONNECTIONS

1. Before reading the story, talk about wanting and waiting for something. Discuss these feelings.
2. After reading the story, discuss whether or not the girl ever gets the earrings. Talk about how and why students reach their conclusions.
3. Speculate on the age of the girl. See if they can find any clues in the story to support their suppositions of age.
4. Give each student one earring. Explain that these are not to wear, but rather are symbols to remind them of a time when they wanted something. Invite them to write about that time. Share writings.

EXTENSIONS

 VOCABULARY/SPELLING:

earrings	pierced	patient	glorious
solar system	premature	inappropriate	old-fashioned
tacky	weird	furthermore	posture
earlobes	bracelet	locket	substitute

LIBRARY CONNECTIONS

Corpus of work:

1. Share other books by Judith Viorst:

   ❖ *Alexander and the Terrible, Horrible, No Good, Very Bad Day*
   ❖ *Alexander, Who Used to Be Rich Last Sunday*
   ❖ *I'll Fix Anthony; If I Were in Charge of the World and other Worries*
   ❖ *My Mama Says There Aren't Any Zombies, Ghosts, Vampires, Creatures, Demons*
   ❖ *Monsters, Fiends, Goblins or Things*
   ❖ *Rosie and Michael; Sunday Morning*
   ❖ *The Tenth Good Thing about Barney*
   ❖ *The Good-Bye Book.*

2. See Sharron L. McElmeel's *Bookpeople: A First Album* for biographical information on Viorst.

   Poetry:

   Share the poem "If I Were in Charge of the World." Invite students to rewrite the poem as if they were the protagonist of *Earrings!*

   Learning the library:

   Help students find the section of the library that contains information on costumes, clothing, customs, cultures.

 SOCIAL STUDIES CONNECTIONS

Students may be interested in researching the customs involving the wearing of earrings, the countries where they are worn, the reasons they are worn, how they are worn, and what they mean.

 ENGLISH/LANGUAGE ARTS CONNECTIONS

Analyzing persuasive techniques:

1. List all the arguments the girl in the story uses to convince her parents to allow her to get her ears pierced.

2. List all the arguments her parents give to justify not allowing her to get her ears pierced.

3. Classify these arguments according to techniques used by advertisers:

   • glittering generalities—using words that sound impressive;
   • emotional appeal—using words that appeal to emotions;
   • testimony—a direct endorsement usually by someone famous;
   • bandwagon—suggest everybody is doing something;
   • logic—sound reasoning;

- Card stacking—giving only one side of the argument;
- Name calling—labeling to avoid the issue;
- Plain folks—attempts to establish a comfort zone.
4. Discuss.

Writing a Persuasive Paper:
Ask each student to assume a stand on pierced ears, earrings, or, by extension, dress codes. Using different colored cards, students write pro arguments on one color, con arguments on the other color. Then they flesh out the arguments on each card. By arranging and rearranging the cards, students can organize their paper so that they can best present the arguments. Students may work in small groups or have conferences. They make any revisions and copy their papers as editorials.

 ART CONNECTIONS

Using lightweight paper, beads, stars, items, and backings for pierced or nonpierced ears from craft stores, students may design and make earrings.

MATHEMATICS/ECONOMICS CONNECTIONS

1. Collect jewelry advertisements from newspapers and magazines. Compare and contrast the cost of like items. Calculate the percentages of reductions. Create word problems based on the information in the ads.
2. Compose a survey with questions centered on the issue of pierced ears. Poll the class, friends, and random students at school. Create a table representing the results of the poll. Change percentages into fractions.

 SCIENCE CONNECTIONS

1. Create a chart of natural materials used in making earrings and other jewelry.
2. Invite a jeweler to class to talk about jewelry making.

👑 **PUBLISHING**

Display all editorials on the bulletin board TAKE A STAND. Display tables, graphs, polls, surveys, ads, art, and other student work around the room.

23

Tacky the Penguin

Helen Lester

Houghton Mifflin Company, 1988

Grade level: 3-7

Artifact: A large construction-paper bow tie

Summary: Tacky, who is different from his graceful companions, proves his uniqueness when the hunters come.

READING/WRITING CONNECTIONS

1. Show students the back cover. Invite comments about the picture.
2. Tacky is different. Show the front cover. Invite speculations about the story.
3. Caution students to listen carefully—they will need to recall specific information afterwards.
4. After the reading, distribute the big bow ties. Hang an enlarged matching bow in a prominent place. Label one bow "Tacky." Explain that on this side they will list the things that apply to Tacky. For example, "wears a flowered shirt." Label the other bow "Others." Explain that on this side they will list the things that apply to Goodly, Lovely, Angel, Neatly, and Perfect. Finally, label the middle or knot of the bow tie "Both." Here students write what Tacky and the other penguins have in common. (The bow tie replicates a Venn Diagram.)
5. Encourage students to think in sets, responding aloud. For example, Tacky marches crazy; the others march in a row; they all march. Tacky does the splashy cannonball; the others dive gracefully; they all dive. When the students understand the procedure, students fill in the bow ties.
6. When they have finished, call on individual students to write a set of characteristics on the enlarged tie until it is full or all characteristics have been exhausted.

EXTENSIONS

VOCABULARY/SPELLING:

tacky	odd	companions	greeted
hearty	graceful	splashy	cannonballs
growly	penguins	dollar	dreadfully

LIBRARY CONNECTIONS

Corpus of work:

Share Lester's

❖ *The Wizard, the Fairy, and the Magic Chicken*

❖ *It Wasn't My Fault*

❖ *A Porcupine Named Fluffy*

❖ *Pookins Gets Her Way*

Additional books:

1. Talk about fiction and nonfiction. Share some nonfiction books about penguins and show students where they can find them in the library.

2. Share other books that allow exploration of comparison and contrast.

❖ William Steig's *Amos & Boris* captures the unlikely friendship of a whale and a mouse;

❖ Sylvia Fair's *The Bedspread* describes how differently two sisters embroider sections of a spread;

❖ Shirley Climo's *The Egyptian Cinderella* —compare and contrast with the classic tale;

❖ Peter Golenbock's *Teammates* tells about Jackie Robinson and Pee Wee Reese;

❖ David McPhail's *Sisters* which compares and contrasts two sisters.

SCIENCE/ π MATHEMATICS CONNECTIONS

1. Introduce lesson with the question: Are penguins birds since they don't fly? Discuss what a species must have to be classified a bird.

2. Measure the height of the Emperor Penguin (the largest). Mark its height with a piece of tape. Measure the height of the Blue Penguin (the smallest). Mark its height with a piece of tape. Have students compute the differences.

3. Discuss why penguins are graceful when diving or when swimming but are awkward on land. Students could research other birds awkward on land.

4. The Flightless Great Auk, a relative of the penguin, is extinct now. Research why. Talk about other birds in danger of extinction.

Writing the Comparison/Contrast (Informative) Paper:

Distribute four sets of index cards (or colored paper cut about that size). Three sets (yellow, green, pink) have three cards in each set. The fourth set (white) has two cards.

1. Students choose three characteristics of Tacky they can write most about, and they write one of those characteristics on each yellow card.
2. Students choose three characteristics of the others that match or make a set with Tacky's characteristics, and they write one of those characteristics on each pink card.
3. Students choose three characteristics of what they have in common to complete the set. They write one of those on each green card. For example:

Yellow/Tacky	Green/Both	Pink/Others
Sang funny songs	Sang	Sang pretty songs
Felt brave	Had feelings	Felt frightened
Greeted heartily	Greeted	Greeted politely

4. Students then write a paragraph on each card. (This is a good time to teach elaboration and to let them do additional reading so they can flesh out the trigger word on each card.)
5. After they finish their three sets, they write an introduction and conclusion on the white set.

Organizing the writing:

1. Tell students that there are several ways to organize a comparison/contrast paper. Ask them to arrange the cards in the way they would like their paper to read.
2. Draw squares on the board to represent paragraphs. As students share their organization schemes, record it on the board. Encourage all alternatives.
3. Teach transitions.
4. Write from cards onto paper.

 PUBLISHING

Construct a pop-up book. Draw rectangles on the folds of oaktag folders to represent Tacky and his companions. Cut the lines perpendicular to the fold. Crease the line parallel to the fold. Bend toward the inside of the folder. Draw or paste pictures on the pop-up block formed when the book is opened. Affix the pages of the comparison/contrast paper in the space provided below the pop-out. Call the display WE LOVE TACKY!

The Gold Coin

Alma Flor Ada
(translated from the Spanish *La Moneda de Oro* by Bernice Randall)

Atheneum, 1991

Grade level: All levels

Artifact: A mint wrapped in gold foil

Summary: A thief determined to steal an old woman's gold coin learns a lesson in true giving.

READING/WRITING CONNECTIONS

1. Begin with two questions. "What would you think if you overheard someone say, 'I must be the richest person in the world'? " Discuss. "What do you think a thief would think?" Discuss.
2. Show the book's cover. Encourage speculation about the meaning of its title and its pictures.
3. After the story, talk about the meaning of "richest person in the world."
4. Distribute the gold coins. Invite students to write about a time when they discovered that something was not what it seemed. Share.

EXTENSIONS

 VOCABULARY/SPELLING:

Juan	poncho	thatch	despair	hoeing
potatoes	hoarse/horse	Dona Josefa	raspy	muttered
wicker	Abuelo	threesome	tensely	mountain
treasure	impatience	harvesting	kernels	traveling
companion	Don Teodosio	amiably	burrowed	lessen
stifling	pair	startling	distressed	ransacked

 **LIBRARY CONNECTIONS**

Other "Golden" Tales:

1. Share other stories that involve gold:
   "The Golden Bird," "The Golden Goose," "The King of the Golden Mountain," "The Giant with the Three Golden Hairs" from *Grimm's Fairy Tales* and "Jack and the Beanstalk," "Little Golden Hood," "The Golden Branch," and "The Golden Goose" from Lang's *The Red Fairy Book*.

2. Invite speculation about why gold plays such a major part in so many stories.
   Other books:
   ❖Katharine Wilson Precek's *Penny in the Road* tells the story of boy who finds an old penny and imagines what life must have been like then.
   ❖Sharon Bell Mathis' *The Hundred Penny Box* (a Newbery Honor Book) captures the love between Michael and his great-great-aunt.
   ❖Margaret Greaves' *The Lucky Coin* brings luck to those who find it.
   Research:
   Help students locate the section in the library that contains information about coins, money, and precious metals.

 **ECONOMICS/MATHEMATICS CONNECTIONS**

1. Guide students in research on the gold standard in the United States. What was it and when and why was it abandoned?

2. Find the "Cash Commodities" in the business section of the newspaper and graph the prices of gold for a week in Hong Kong, London, Paris, Frankfurt, Zurich, and New York.

3. Make a chart of the gold coins listed in the newspaper (e.g. maple leaf, Mexican peso, American eagle, Krugerrand, and so forth), and graph the prices of these gold coins for a week.

4. Invite a numismatist to speak.

5. Help students develop a written explanation of the gold *carat*.

6. Have students write in their own words what Euclid meant by "the golden section of a line" (the principle that a line may be divided into two segments such that the ratio of the shorter segment and the longer segment are equal to the ratio of the longer segment to the whole line).

SOCIAL STUDIES CONNECTIONS

1. State coinage originated in Lydia in the seventh century B.C. Ask students to construct a time line showing the development of money throughout the world.

2. Let students write to the United States Mint, 633 3rd Street NW, Washington, DC

20220, for information on how money is made.

3. After students research the GOLD RUSH in America's history. Watch Charlie Chaplin's film *The Gold Rush*. Discuss how the discovery of gold in California affected the western movement.

ENGLISH/LANGUAGE ARTS CONNECTIONS

Idioms:

Working in groups, create a *comic book* that literally depicts the following idioms about gold. Reserve a place in the book for the idiomatic meaning of each.

> gold-digger
> good as gold
> to be a gold-mine
> worth one's weight in gold
> have a heart of gold
> crock of gold at the end of the rainbow
> fool's gold
> gold bricking
> all he touches turns to gold
> Golden Age
> Golden Wedding

Finding Sources:

Working in groups, research the following literary allusions:

> "All that glitters is not gold."
>> (Shakespeare, *The Merchant of Venice*, act 2, scene 7)
> "But al thing which that shyneth as the gold
> Nit nat gold, as that I have herd it told."
>> (Chaucer, *Canterbury Tales*, "The Canon's Yeoman's Tale")
> "To worship the golden calf"
>> (Bible, Exodus 32: 1-14)
> "The Golden Fleece"
>> (Greek myth; one source is Edith Hamilton's *Mythology*)
> "The Golden Number"
>> (Roman and Alexandrian calendars; to find, check the *Book of Common Prayer* tables to find Easter Day)
> "I have a sty here, Chilax. I have no gold to cure it."
>> (Beaumont and Fletcher, *The Mad Lover*, act 5, scene 4)

PUBLISHING

Cover a bulletin board with gold paper. Display all the students' research and writing. Call it THE GOLDEN HORDE!

The Art Lesson

Tomie dePaola

G. P. Putnam's Sons, 1989

Grade level: All levels

Artifact: A crayon

Summary: Tommy learns to be creative and to compromise.

READING/WRITING CONNECTIONS

1. Invite talk about drawing and art in school. Discuss why some people like to draw and others seem shy about their work. Talk about creativity, discussing the difference between tracing and composing. Discuss Saul Bass's idea of creativity as "looking at one thing and seeing another" (quoted in David Sohn's *Film: The Creative Eye*). Talk about the difference between doing someone else's picture and doing your own.
2. Ask students if they know what they want to be when they grow up.
3. Show the cover. Invite speculation about the book by studying the cover. Invite predictions about what might happen.
4. After reading the book, talk about those predictions. Discuss how people do things they enjoy. Talk about Jack and Herbie and Jeannie and what they might grow up to become.
5. Give each student a crayon. Have them draw a picture of their choice and then write about a time when they were forced to copy what someone else did. Share.

EXTENSIONS

 VOCABULARY/SPELLING:

artist	favorite	turtles	cartwheels
barber shop	Nana	Irish	Nana-Fall-River
Italian	Aunt Clo	carpenters	kindergarten
smock	Crayola™	blue-violet	turquoise
red-orange	monitor	Pilgrim	whispered

 **LIBRARY CONNECTIONS**

Corpus of Work:

Arrange a book exhibit of dePaola's extensive corpus of work. For more information, see Sharron L. McElmeel's *An Author A Month (for Pennies)*.

Other art books:

1. In the following set of fiction books, the paintings almost come alive. These are wonderful to use along with art prints. Invite the students to pretend to enter the paintings or imagine something coming out of the painting alive:
   - ✛James Mayhew's *Katie's Picture Show*
   - ✛Jon Agee's *The Incredible Painting of Felix Clousseau*
   - ✛Donald Carrick's *Morgan and the Artist*
   - ✛Mike Dickinson's *Smudge*
   - ✛Mark Strand's *Rembrandt Takes a Walk*
   - ✛Johnny Alcorn's *Rembrandt's Beret*
   - ✛Ewa Zadrzynska's *The Girl with a Watering Can*.

2. In these fiction books, the protagonists all share a creative dream:
   - ✛Rex Harley's *Mary's Tiger*
   - ✛Denys Cazet's *Frosted Glass*
   - ✛Leo Lionni's *Matthew's Dream*

3. Two interesting books focus on Henri Rousseau's "The Sleeping Gypsy." Brown and Brown use it as one of the masterpieces viewed when *Visiting the Art Museum*, whereas Geoffrey Patterson uses it as the start of his fable *The Lion and the Gypsy*.

4. The following books are biographical nonfiction. The last four listed are part of the "First Impressions" Introductions to Art series:
   - ✛Gladys S. Blizzard's *Come Look with Me: Enjoying Art with Children*
   - ✛Mike Venezia's *Mary Cassatt*
   - ✛Leslie Sills' *Inspirations: Stories About Women Artists*
   - ✛Greenberg and Jordan's *The Painter's Eye*
   - ✛Richard Meryman's *Andrew Wyeth*
   - ✛Susan E. Meyer's *Mary Cassatt*
   - ✛Howard Greenfeld's *Marc Chagall*
   - ✛Richard McLanathan's *Leonardo da Vinci*.
   - ✛See also Christina Bjork's delightful combination of fact and fiction in *Linnea in Monet's Garden*.

5. You might also use Thomas Locker's *The Young Artist*, the tale of a how a young artist deals with the challenge of painting noblewomen not as they are but as they want the world to see them, and Karen Ackerman's *Araminta's Paint Box*, a quaint story of the adventures of a paint box amid America's westward movement.

ENGLISH/LANGUAGE ARTS CONNECTIONS

Art to Introduce Literature:

Use Tomie dePaola's *Bonjour, Mr. Satie* to introduce high school students to the "Lost Generation." This book captures the spirit of the time as well as all the known creative folk who gathered at Gertrude Stein's salon.

Art to prompt writing:

1. Students use art prints to evoke a memory or experience for writing.
2. They can mentally enter the picture and interact with what they find.
3. They can look at a picture and create a story about what they see.
4. They can describe a picture.
5. They can compare and/or contrast one art work with another.
6. They can persuade someone to purchase the artwork.

 SOCIAL STUDIES CONNECTIONS

1. Use *Bonjour, Mr. Satie* to begin work on the World War I era (1914-1918), the war itself, and the social disorder following it.
2. Introduce the period under study with art. Discuss whether art influences what happens in the world or vice versa. For examples, consider the artistic movements of Impressionism, Expressionism, Realism, Romanticism, Surrealism. What milieu created or fostered these movements?

π MATHEMATICS/ SCIENCE CONNECTIONS

1. Investigate the beginning of things as described at the outset of deLarminat's *Vassily Kandinsky: Sky Blue*, for example: cells, globules, seeds, pollen, moons, paint. Challenge students to rewrite in scientific terms what is being said.
3. Create a grid on laminate. Place the grid over a picture. Using a proportion formula, enlarge one square per student from the grid. Each student then reproduces one section of the painting from the grid. When they are finished, mount the grids, thereby reproducing a larger version of the entire picture.

PUBLISHING

Share at least one thing composed during this art lesson with a CREATIVITY AND ME DAY.

26

Volcano: The Eruption and Healing of Mount St. Helens

Patricia Lauber

Bradbury Press, 1986
(Newbery Honor Book)

Artifact: A tiny piece of lava rock (pumice)

Summary: Through colored illustrations and photographs taken by researchers, scientists, and naturalists and through accurate prose, the reader experiences Mount St. Helens' eruption and its aftermath.

READING/WRITING CONNECTIONS

1. While sharing the title and author, show the jacket cover. Tell the students that what they see is Mount St. Helens two years after its big eruption on May 18, 1980. Point out that even as the picture was taken, St. Helens was giving off gas and ash. Call their attention to the dome in the center of the crater, which continued to grow as eruptions added lava to it.

2. As you read, stop frequently so that the full benefits of this photographic essay may be savored. (This book might best be read in two installments—chapters 1 and 2; chapters 3, 4, and 5.)

3. Distribute pieces of lava. After students examine the pieces, invite them to follow the reporters' formula and write about *when* and *where* the pieces may have been found, *how* they were found, *who* found them, *what* happened after finding them, and *why* it happened? Share.

EXTENSIONS

 VOCABULARY/SPELLING:

eruption	mantel	magma	molten	pumice	lava
conduits	geologists	earthquake	avalanche	Fahrenheit	sandblasted
molts	scorched	mudflows	colonizers	bacteria	fungi
spores	mantle	plates	plateau	volcano	dormant

LIBRARY CONNECTIONS

1. Awards:
   Discuss why this book was awarded the Newbery Medal.

2. Index:
   Study the index of this book. Demonstrate how to use the index by looking up the words in the preceding vocabulary/spelling list.

3. Map study:
   Find the Cascade Range on the map of the United States and on a world map or globe. Interpret the information on the maps on pages 2, 7, and 53.

4. Research teams:
   Divide the class into two teams, the "Geologists" and the "Vulcanologists"
   • Each member on TEAM A (geologists) chooses one topic from the following list to research. Encourage the use of all resources in the library. The geologists' report might consist solely of illustrations (transparencies, charts, diagrams) demonstrating how the object of their research works.

volcanoes	craters	lava and lava plugs
geysers	earthquakes	avalanches

   • Each member on TEAM B (Vulcanologists) chooses one of the following volcanoes to research: Mauna Kea, Hawaii; Ojos del Salado, Andes (South America); Paricutin, Mexico; Tambora, Indonesia; Bezymianny, Russia; Mount Pelée, Martinique. After their initial research, have the group members compare similarities and differences.
   • Students prepare their summaries as if they have been invited to share their findings on a five minute spot on television.

5. Other books:
   ❖*Everybody Needs a Rock* by Byrd Baylor. Students create a "Rule 11" to fit their lava rock.

   ❖*Whose Footprints?* by Masayuki Yabuucki. After looking at pages thirty-six and thirty-seven in *Volcano,* showing where scientists found tracks of animals in the ash, younger students can have fun as you read Yabuuchi's book by pretending to be scientists identifying animals by their tracks. They can make a "tracks" book, perhaps by stamping them with stamps that have different animal prints.

ENGLISH/LANGUAGE ARTS CONNECTIONS

Note taking:
As scientists, students keep a "Volcano Log." On the left page, they write facts about the volcano they choose, such as its height, site, number of eruptions, and size of its crater. On the right page, they explore their feelings about those facts, such as: awe at its magnificence.

Cause and effect:

Students fold a sheet of paper in half. On the top half, they list causes such as how and why volcanoes form; how and why they erupt. On the bottom half, they list what happens after an eruption. Using this as prewriting, they compose a cause-and-effect paper.

 SCIENCE CONNECTIONS

1. **Group work:**

   Students work in groups to discover more information on: building a miniature volcano; finding the San Andreas fault; gurgling undersea volcanoes; Pompeii, the buried wonder city; volcanoes on other planets; and the Richter Scale— measuring earthquakes. Use chapter 16 "Volcanoes" and chapter 17 "Rocks" in *Science through Children's Literature* by Carol M. Butzow and John W. Butzow for dozens of activities.

2. **Experiments with pumice:**

   Test the hypothesis that rocks can float. Test ways to use pumice as an abrasive.

3. **Geology and Petrology:**

   Divide the class into two groups: "geologists" and "petrologists."

   • Those designated "geologists" investigate where volcanoes exist and why they exist there, how long they have been there, and if they are still active or if they are extinct.

   • Those designated "petrologists" classify rocks by where they came from, what they are made of, how they are formed, and what makes them distinctive.

 PUBLISHING

EXPLOSION DAY! Display all the work completed during the volcano unit. Play the explosive *Music for the Royal Fireworks* by George Frederic Handel as background.

27

Lincoln:
    A Photobiography

Russell Freedman

Clarion Books, 1987
Newbery Winner

Grade level: 5-12

Artifact: A Lincoln penny

Summary: Photographs and prose tell the life of Lincoln.

READING/WRITING CONNECTIONS

1. Show and discuss the portrait of Lincoln on the cover of the book. Invite the students to describe Lincoln. Then read his description of himself on page 1. Talk about what they know and remember learning about Lincoln.
2. Show a sampling of pictures throughout the book, for example, the log cabin (8), Lincoln and Mary Lincoln (26), the series of Lincoln portraits (64-65), the Gettysburg Address (103), later portraits (116-117), the president lying in state (131).
3. Give each student a penny. Discuss Lincoln's portrait on the penny. Compare to book's cover.
4. Read aloud the first chapter "The Mysterious Mr. Lincoln."
5. Write on the board or overhead projector the following quotation taken from "A Lincoln Sampler" (135): "Writing, the art of communicating thoughts to the mind through the eye, is the great invention of the world. . . enabling us to converse with the dead, the absent, and the unborn, at all distances of time and space." (*From lecture before the Springfield Library Association, February 22, 1860.*) Read it aloud. Talk about it. Then invite students to write their interpretation of what Lincoln said about writing. Share written responses in small group.

EXTENSIONS

 VOCABULARY/SPELLING:

countenance	wreathed	animation	folks	reticent
legendary	homespun	diplomats	patronized	eloquent
emancipator	rollicking	melancholy	bungling	defy

LIBRARY CONNECTIONS

1. *Lincoln: A Photobiography* won the Newbery Award in 1988. Discuss why it was so honored.
2. Check *Bookpeople: A Second Album* by Sharron L. McElmeel for biographical information on Russell Freedman.

   Gather other books by Freedman. Discuss non-fiction writing.
   - ❖*Buffalo Hunt*
   - ❖*Children of the Wild West*
   - ❖*Cowboys of the Wild West*
   - ❖*Immigrant Kids*
   - ❖*Dinosaurs and Their Young*
   - ❖*Farm Babies*
   - ❖*Franklin Delano Roosevelt: A Biography*
   - ❖*Rattlesnakes*
   - ❖*Indian Chief*
3. Using library reference books and a photocopier, create an illustrated timeline for Lincoln's life that will cover an entire wall or several walls. Groups or individuals can concentrate on segments of his life to research.
4. Use *Lincoln* to show and discuss with students the placement and function not only of the title, copyright, and dedication pages, but also the table of contents (called simply "Contents" in this book), the appendices of ("A Lincoln Sampler," "In Lincoln's Footsteps," "Books About Lincoln," "Acknowledgments and Picture Credits" [this is an apt time to discuss attribution], and the index.

 SOCIAL STUDIES/ LANGUAGE ARTS CONNECTIONS

1. Group projects and letter writing:

   Divide class into four groups. Each group decides on a group project. For example, a map of Lincoln's life; a three-dimensional depiction of Ford's Theatre; or a dramatization of the Lincoln-Douglas debates. Then they choose the appropriate place to write for information. As a group, they compose one letter. (This is a good time to teach the proper letter-writing form for this type of letter.) Addresses are given in Freedman's book for the Springfield Visitors Bureau, the Lincoln Heritage Trail Foundation, the Gettysburg National Military Park, and Ford's Theatre.
2. Research:

   Students create a presidential two-page spread, using as a model the book *The Buck Stops Here: The Presidents of the United States* by Alice Provensen. Students synthesize information they have researched to fit this format. Display the two-page spreads.
3. Writing autobiography, biography, memoir, or portrait:

Using ideas from Richard Beach's *Writing about Ourselves and Others*, William Zinsser's *Inventing the Truth,* and/or Donald Graves' *Investigate Nonfiction*, excite the students about writing a photoautobiography, photobiography, photomemoir, or photoportrait.

4. Text Renderings of "The Gettysburg Address":

Part of the beauty of "The Gettysburg Address" is its rhetoric. Help students see how parallelism and the repetition of words or phrases that have similar grammatical structures illuminate meaning.

Group students. Assign a section of the address to each group. Each group practices rendering its section by repeating words or phrases they consider important or especially meaningful; reading some lines together as a group and others as individuals; rearranging; and omitting. Students may not add any new words. Each section presents its rendering.

 ART CONNECTIONS

Crafting portraits:

Divide students into pairs. Using an opaque projector for backlighting, students trace a profile portrait of their partners on round piece of copper-colored paper. Mount these enlarged "pennies" around the room.

 MUSIC/LITERATURE CONNECTIONS

1. Develop a choral speaking program around "I Hear America Speaking" by Walt Whitman. Use *Fun with Choral Speaking* by Rose Marie Anthony. Make a tape of the students' rendition.

2. Share excerpts from Carl Sandburg's biography *Abraham Lincoln*.

3. Play *Lincoln Portrait* by Aaron Copeland. One version has Henry Fonda narrating (CBS NK 42431); another features Katharine Hepburn (Telarc CD 80117).

 PUBLISHING

Create a PRESIDENTIAL PARADE. Display all books, writings, portraits, projects on Lincoln and/or on other presidents.

Black Star, Bright Dawn

Scott O'Dell

Houghton Mifflin Company, 1988

Grade level: 6-12

Artifact: A 10-inch black construction-paper star

Summary: Bright Dawn takes her father's place in the Iditarod dogsled race and faces its challenges from Anchorage to Nome, Alaska.

READING/WRITING CONNECTIONS

1. Read the dedication, explain the title, and show the map as you describe the Iditarod race.
2. Discuss the characteristics of people who would risk the Iditarod.
3. Introduce the characters of Oteg and Kathy Logan.
4. Read chapter 10 in which Oteg tells the story of the Raven. Talk about his story and how and why the Eskimo's world was filled with such explanations of mysteries. Compare this to the animism of the early Greeks, the notion that all nature was alive with spirits.
5. Students cut stars out of construction paper. Using Oteg's explanation of how the Raven got its "caw" as their model, students write a *pourquoi* tale explaining how the lead dog came to be marked with a black star. Share.

EXTENSIONS

 **VOCABULARY/SPELLING: Compound words**

checkpoint	riverbank	checkpoint	snowhouse
soapstone	sunset	everywhere	himself
something	tailfeathers	doorway	nightfall

LIBRARY CONNECTIONS

1. Create a display of a corpus of O'Dell's work:
   ✣ *Alexandra*
   ✣ *The Amethyst Ring*
   ✣ *The Black Pearl*
   ✣ *The Captive*
   ✣ *Carlotta*
   ✣ *The Castle in the Sea*
   ✣ *The Cruise of the Arctic Star*
   ✣ *Dark Canoe*
   ✣ *The Feathered Serpent*
   ✣ *Island of the Blue Dolphins*
   ✣ *Sarah Bishop*
   ✣ *Sing Down the Moon*
   ✣ *The Spanish Smile*
   ✣ *Streams to the River, River to the Sea: A Novel of Sacagawea*
   ✣ *Zia*

2. Talk about O'Dell's awards:
   Newbery Medalist, three-time Newbery Honor Book winner, recipient of the Hans Christian Andersen Medal, winner of the deGrummond and Regina medals, two-time winner of the German Jugendbuchpreis, and ALA Notable Books winner. Collect other biographical information about O'Dell.

3. Write a review of one of O'Dell's books. Compare your review with published reviews.

4. Share other books on Eskimos, Alaska, and the Arctic:
   Alexander and Alexander's *An Eskimo Family,* and *The Eskimos*
   ✣ Andrews' *Very Last First Time*
   ✣ Ekoomiak's *Arctic Memories* (written in both English and Inukitut)
   ✣ Freuchen's *Book of Eskimos*
   ✣ George's *Julie of the Wolves,* and *Water Sky*
   ✣ Gill's *The Alaska Mother Goose*
   ✣ Gubok's *The Art of the Eskimo*
   ✣ Houston's *Akavak, The White Archer,* and *Wolf Run*
   ✣ Meyer's *Eskimos: Growing Up in a Changing Culture*
   ✣ Paulsen's *Dogsong ,*and *Wood-Song*
   ✣ Pinkwater's *Aunt Lulu*
   ✣ Purdy and Sandak's *Eskimos: A Civilization Project Book*
   ✣ Rasmussen's *Beyond the High Hills/A Book of Eskimo Poems*
   ✣ Williams and Major's *The Secret Language of Snow*
   ✣ Yue and Yue's *The Igloo*

 ENGLISH/LANGUAGE ARTS/  ART CONNECTIONS

1. Locate articles on Eskimos, their environment, and their culture in past issues of magazines, especially *National Geographic*. Make a pictorial essay for classroom display to help explain Eskimo mythology.
2. Create a slide presentation of Eskimo art (slides are often available for a small fee through museums, or they may be made from original art). Pictures used on an opaque projector may be substituted for slides.
3. Tell your version of an Eskimo myth. Choose from the creation myth of "Senda" or "The Old Woman of the Sea," or from the myths about caves, animals, birds, the Shaman or Angakok, taboos, the sun, "The Bewitched Wife," death. Use sound effects during the presentation.
4. Reenact an Eskimo poem such as the one at the end of Paulsen's *Dogsong*.
5. Compare and contrast pre-twentieth century and contemporary Eskimo art.

π MATHEMATICS CONNECTIONS

Research the catenary principle:

Construct a miniature igloo from marshmallows or sugar cubes to demonstrate this principle. Scale to size. Give the dimensions. Calculate how many blocks of snow it would take to really build it.

 SCIENCE CONNECTIONS

1. Study the principles of insulation. Discuss how to apply these principles to the clothing of the Eskimo. Compare the ideas from this discussion with instances of actual use in other clothing, found through research.
2. Study the phenomena of the aurora borealis and permafrost. Discuss how these affected Eskimo culture, religion, clothing, lodgings.
3. Create an information booklet about the plants and animals of the arctic regions.

 SOCIAL STUDIES CONNECTIONS

1. Eskimo life and culture:

Show the following films available through the National Film Board of Canada:
  ❖ *How to Build an Igloo,*
  ❖ *Kenojuak: Eskimo Artist*
  ❖ *The Living Stone*

2. Documentary film study:

View Robert Flaherty's documentary, *Nanook of the North*. Made in 1922, the film provides an honest impression of Eskimo life, although much ingenuity and staging went into its production.

ART CONNECTIONS

Whittle an animal from a bar of Ivory™ soap as the Eskimos might have from walrus tusks, bone, or more recently from soapstone (steatite).

PUBLISHING

Create a display ESKIMO PRINTS with the students' stories, pictures, art, books, and articles. Celebrate by making and eating some Eskimo ice cream described in the book, or by eating Eskimo "pies" (ice cream sandwiches).

29

Bearstone

Will Hobbs

Atheneum, 1989

Grade level: 6-12

Artifact: A clay fetish.

Summary: A rite of passage story of a troubled Indian boy, an elderly rancher, and a turquoise bearstone.

READING/WRITING CONNECTIONS

1. Write the word *fetish* on the board, overhead, or chart. Discuss its meaning. Ask if students have ever seen a fetish. Explain that a fetish can either be natural or man-made, and that it is usually associated with characteristic of what it represents (animal fetishes bring good luck in hunting, for example).

2. Since fetishes are often carried in "medicine bags" and are always respected, show a pouch containing a fetish. Tell about that fetish: where it was found, how you got it, why you have kept it.

3. Look at the book's jacket. Speculate about the relationship of the young Indian and the bear.

4. Before reading, provide Cloyd's background. Explain that the group home where his tribe had sent him sends him to work for an old rancher. Early in the novel, Cloyd explores some cliffs near the ranch. Begin reading with, "Cloyd sprang to the ledge." in chapter 3. Continue to chapter's end.

5. Distribute lumps of clay. Students fashion fetishes of an animal or object with which they identify. Distribute index cards or squares of paper on which students write brief descriptions of their fetishes and why they chose that animal or object. Share. Display fetishes and index cards in room.

EXTENSIONS

 **VOCABULARY/SPELLING:**

handholds   duffel bag   tendons   quiver   tremble

| summoned | shuffling | yucca | wriggled | shards |
| turquoise | snout | Utes | journey | twilight |

 LIBRARY CONNECTIONS

1. About the author:

   Share some biographical information about Will Hobbs. He grew up in Alaska, Texas, and California and now lives in Colorado. Encourage students to think what they would ask Hobbs about *Bearstone, Changes in Latitudes,* or *Downriver*. Do a book talk on these two latter books to encourage students to read them.

2. Related books:

   Cloyd is of the Weminuche Utes. Use *The Village of Blue Stone* by Stephen Trimble for information about the people called Anasazi and how fetishes figured into their culture for comparisons. Use also Terri Cohlene's *Turquoise Boy: A Navajo Legend*.

3. Learning the library:

   Help students find information on other tribes and cultures and their fetishes. Map these tribes and surround the map with pictures of fetishes from each tribe. Then compare the variety of fetishes with modern-day symbols such as worry stones, rabbit's feet, and others.

ENGLISH/LANGUAGE ARTS CONNECTIONS

1. Rite-of-Passage theme:

   Working in groups, brainstorm other books (classic and contemporary) as well as films and television shows that have a rite-of passage theme. Discuss the timeless quality of this theme.

2. Using the thesaurus:

   Find synonyms for the word *fetish*.

3. Quicky Research:

   Find one fact about fetishes used by different tribes or different cultures. Share. Decide if modern people have fetishes. Discuss how meanings of words can change; for example, we sometimes use the word to connote an obsession. ("She has a fetish about her telephone.")

4. Letter writing:

   Write a letter from Cloyd to Walter about the incident of the peach trees. Exchange with someone in the room. Write Walter's response.

5. Journal entry:

   Write a journal entry describing your feelings about the peach tree incident. Share.

6. Tall tales:

   Walter was always making up tall tales. Tell a tall tale Walter would enjoy reading or hearing.

7. Newspaper:

Walter liked to read the *Mining Gazette*. Working in groups, write an article or draw a cartoon for that newspaper. Keep in mind the geographical area and the times.

8. Persuasive writing:

Write an editorial convincing people not to hunt illegally. Think of yourself as Cloyd; think of your audience as Rusty.

9. Writing a chapter:

Write chapter 23 for the book.

 MUSIC CONNECTIONS

Play *The Ancient Ones*, a flute solo performed by Pamela Copus in the Anasazi Indian ruins of Chaco Canyon, New Mexico. Students write or draw what comes to mind as they listen. After sharing, read the information provided with the tape. Discuss the connection between Cloyd's experience in the cave of the Ancient Ones and the tape.

 SOCIAL STUDIES CONNECTIONS

1. Burial rites and rituals:

Cloyd discovered a burial place of the Ancient Ones. Research burial rites and rituals of other tribes and cultures. Be prepared to share with the class.

2. Cave paintings:

Look up information on cave paintings. Record several interesting facts about these paintings. Connect them with the novel.

3. The Utes:

Read about the Utes. Evaluate the accuracy of the information Hobbs used in the novel. Draw conclusions about fact in fiction.

4. Map making:

Create a map of Cloyd's journey throughout the book. Begin at the hospital room; end on Walter's ranch.

5. Research:

Trace Walter's interest in gold from the California Gold Rush of 1848 or from other gold rushes such as those in Australia (1851-1853), South Africa (1884) and Canada (1897-1898).

 PUBLISHING

Gather in small groups for PEACH DAY. Distribute peaches (halves or quarters will do). Spray the room with peach scent. Discuss what peaches represent. Students share one of their activities.

 **30**

Dr. JAC

Hatchet

Gary Paulsen

Bradbury Press, 1987
Newbery Honor Book

Grade level: 6-8

Artifact: Some item from student's pocket or purse

Summary: Because his parents are divorced, Brian must fly to the Canadian wilderness to visit his father. The plane crashes and Brian learns much about survival.

READING/WRITING CONNECTIONS

1. Divide students into groups. Students contribute one or several things out of their pockets or purses as part of the group's assets.
2. Invite the students to imagine they are on a plane that crashes in the wilderness of Canada, leaving them stranded as a group.
3. Students analyze their assets in terms of survival. Share.
4. Introduce the book. Begin the reading from chapter 5 with, "The trouble, Brian thought..." and continue to "*You* are the best thing you have." Discuss the act of thinking as an asset.
5. Students write their reactions to what they find in their pockets and purses as means of survival. Discuss what people need to survive certain situations (for example, earthquakes, floods, getting caught in an elevator) and what they need, in general, to survive. Share.

EXTENSIONS

 VOCABULARY/SPELLING:

drum	positive	motivated	pitiful
fingernail	hatchet	tennis	windbreaker
digital	valuable	obvious	stranded

 **LIBRARY CONNECTIONS**

1. Corpus of work:

Share other books by the author:

❖ *The Boy Who Owned the School*

❖ *Canyons*

❖ *Dancing Carl*

❖ *The Cookcamp The Voyage of the Frog*

❖ *The Crossing*

❖ *Dogsong*

❖ *The Island*

❖ *The Night the White Deer Died*

❖ *Popcorn Days & Buttermilk Nights*

❖ *Sentries*

❖ *Tracker*

❖ *The Winter Room*

❖ *Woodsong*

Point out that three of Paulsen's books are Newbery Honor Books: *Dogsong, Hatchet,* and *The Winter Room.*

2. Learning the library:

• Demonstrate how to find areas in the library where students can find information on Canada and its wilderness areas.

• Use atlases to locate the area where Brian crashed.

• Explain how they can use *Facts on File* for statistics on divorce, on plane crashes, on most anything.

3. Related books:

Have students locate other survival stories in the periodicals section of the library and read them. Together prepare a chart listing human characteristics that helped people survive within the various environments described.

 ENGLISH/LANGUAGE ARTS CONNECTIONS

1. Talk Show:

Create a television talk show panel with Brian as the guest. Students play the parts of other panel members, the host, the audience.

An alternative panel may be comprised of students playing Brian, Mom, Dad, Perpich, and the fur-buyer pilot who found Brian. Video tape the talk shows, if possible. Discuss.

2. Interviews and related writing:

Divide students into pairs. One becomes Brian, the other an investigative reporter who interviews him. Encourage the reporter to be creative and try to get an angle (perhaps the reporter could suggest sabotage of some kind). Afterward, the reporter writes his or her article; "Brian" writes his reactions in a journal. Share. Then talk about the ethics involved in good reporting, looking at the facts not for sensationalism. Talk about "yellow journalism." Discuss truth and ethics in the press.

3. Keeping logs:

Brian was in the wilderness 54 days. Working in small groups, review the novel with a close reading then create a log of Brian's activities each day.

4. Carpe Diem:

Read Margaret Wise Brown's *David's Little Indian*. Discuss the concept of *carpe diem*, "seize the day." As a class brainstorm connections between *carpe diem* and Brian's survival, for example, "Day of the First Rabbit." Find examples of carpe diem in literature.

5. Sequel:

Brian's Winter, another Paulsen novel, takes the Brain Robeson of *Hatchet* and writes out of the hypothesis "What if Brian hadn't been rescued?" Discuss the hyptothesis as a way to motivate student to read the novel.

 SCIENCE CONNECTIONS

1. Categorizing:

Create a chart with categories for the foods Brian found. Share by explaining your method of categorizing.

2. Research:

Research other edibles that might be available in the Canadian wilderness. Present to class in a creative way.

3. Problem solving:

Brian asks, "What makes fire?" Write a "Survival Booklet for Beginners." Include how to make a fire, what to do for insect bites, and solutions for other problems Brian encountered.

4. Making and proving a hypothesis:

Divide students into groups. Distribute strips of butcher paper (half the usual width). Students create a "Hypothesis Flow Chart" explaining their reasoning on why the plane moved after its crash and their attempts to prove their hypothesis scientifically.

 SOCIAL STUDIES CONNECTIONS

Study a map of Canada. Draw the map and pinpoint the area where Brian went down.

π MATHEMATICS CONNECTIONS

1. Numbers:

   Brian didn't know the meaning of the number (160) he saw on the lighted dial of the plane. He thought it could be actual miles per hour, kilometers, or the speed of the moving plane through the air. Brainstorm reasons to support each choice. In groups prove the correct choice mathematically.

2. Distances:

   Draw a bird's-eye-view map of the Canadian wilderness. Use lightweight paper to map out the general area. Then use fine-point markers to label the places Brian used. Walk off an area of the classroom. Use as an approximate to measure distances between the places Brian used. Apply those approximates to Brian's walks from place to place. Be sure to include a scale and a key on your map.

3. Interpreting graphs:

   Graph and then compute the trajectory of the plane as it crashed.

 PUBLISHING

Plan a Welcome Back party for Brian. Decorate the room by displaying projects. Choose something to read.

31

Dr. JAC

Bridge to Terabithia

Katherine Paterson

Thomas Y. Crowell , 1977

KATHERINE PATERSON

BRIDGE TO TERABITHIA

Illustrated by Donna Diamond

Grade level: 4-8

Artifact: A piece of rope, preferably frayed at the ends

Summary: Jess, a 10-year-old boy in rural Virginia, becomes friends with Leslie, a girl who understands him and helps extend his creative world. Together they create Terabithia, their own fantasy land. Leslie dies trying to reach Terabithia during a storm, and Jess must deal with grief and loss.

READING/WRITING CONNECTIONS

1. Read the title, author, and dedication. Invite speculation about why David wanted Lisa's name included. Discuss the meaning of the word *banzai*. (See *Gates of Excellence* or *The Horn Book,* August 1978 for Paterson's reasoning.)
2. Discuss friends:
   Why we have them, what we share with them, and how we make them. Discuss girls and boys being friends.
3. Either read through the book chapter-by-chapter or read chapter 4, "Rulers of Terabithia."
4. Distribute the pieces of rope. Students write about an imaginary place where they may go using this piece of *enchanted* rope. Share.

EXTENSIONS

 VOCABULARY/SPELLING:

forehead	gorgeous	thrumming	shimmering
cross-legged	melodic	prissily	hippies
shinnying	gymnasium	patiently	wrestled
suspiciously	intoxicated	dolphin	insufficiencies

 **LIBRARY CONNECTIONS**

1. Corpus of work:

   Share other books by Paterson. Consult *Bookpeople: A Second Album* by Sharron L. McElmeel for selected titles and biographical information.

2. Related books by Paterson:

   Show students Paterson's *Gates of Excellence*. Read "Laying the First Plank" which contains her first draft of *Bridge to Terabithia*. Read "From the Newbery Medal Acceptance," the speech she gave in 1978 for the book. Share excerpts from The *Spying Heart* so students can see the breadth of the author's work and hear some of her commentary on reading and writing books.

3. Afterward:

   After hearing some of this additional information, discuss what part readers might find interesting. Invite students to write that as an afterward to *Bridge to Terabithia*.

4. Related books about friends:

   Share many other books about friends:

   ✤Karen Ackerman's *The Tin Heart* places friendship against the backdrop of the Civil War.

   ✤James Marshall's *The Cut-Ups* presents the funny side of friendship.

   ✤Judith Viorst's *Rosie and Michael* tells what friends like about each other, even the bad things.

   ✤Alana White's *Come Next Spring* deals with change and friendship.

   ✤Elizabeth Winthrop's *Lizzie and Harold* proves boys and girls can be friends.

5. Create a chart showing the book title; what the crisis in friendship was; whether the crisis was resolved (*yes* or *no*); and why or why not. Draw conclusions as a class about various types of friendships.

 ENGLISH/LANGUAGE ARTS CONNECTIONS

1. **Symbolism:**

   Discuss the symbolism of bridges. Play the Simon and Garfunkel song "Bridge Over Troubled Water." Discuss it in relation to the book.

2. **Allusions:**

   Teach allusions by using those in the following:

   ✤*Moby Dick*
   ✤*The Chronicles of Narnia*
   ✤*Hamlet*
   ✤*Star Trek*
   ✤*The Ten Commandments* (film)
   ✤Abraham Lincoln
   ✤Socrates

❖the Bible

❖Dear Abby

❖the coyote in *Road Runner* cartoons.

3. Comparison/contrast:

Write a paper comparing and contrasting Jess and Leslie. Write a paper comparing and contrasting yourself with a friend.

4. Field trip:

Take a field trip to a local bridge. Log feelings when approaching it, looking at it, and from it. Log what is seen from various angles. Look for small details. Jot down any stories you have heard related to the bridge. Relate any cautions you have heard about bridges.

5. Adverbs:

Paterson is the master of the precise adverb. Students identify adverbs on a given page then practice using adverbs in their writing.

6. Epitaphs and Eulogies:

Write an epitaph or eulogy for Leslie. Share.

 SOCIAL STUDIES CONNECTIONS

Rituals of death:

Discuss feelings about a family member, a friend, or a pet that has died. (Be sensitive to students who might have suffered a recent loss.) Research funeral rites, cremation, beliefs surrounding death, or cultural and religious views of death. Study the stages of grief. Identify how Jess manifested those stages.

 ART CONNECTIONS

Drawing and painting:

Draw Terabithia the way you think Jess or Leslie saw it, or draw it the way you imagine it. Paint the drawing using some or all of the 24 colors you think were in the box of watercolors Leslie gave Jess for Christmas.

π MATHEMATICS CONNECTIONS

Measurement:

Construct a bridge using any materials you choose. Using the measurements of the bridge and the principles of ratio, scale the bridge and draw plans as it would have to be to span certain widths, such as a 200-foot expanse, a 1000 foot expanse, and so forth

MUSIC CONNECTIONS

Songs in the book:

Sing the songs Miss Edmunds taught the students: "My Beautiful Balloon," "This Land Is Your Land," "Free to Be You and Me," "Blowing in the Wind," and "God Bless America."

 PUBLISHING

SHARE WITH A FRIEND DAY! Each student brings a coffee can filled with things to share with a friend just as Jess and Leslie shared the contents of the three-pound coffee can they kept at Terabithia. Students may fill their coffee cans with dried fruit and crackers, but they should also include the work they did and information they discovered during their study of the book.

Miracle at the Plate

Matt Christopher

Little, Brown and Company, 1967

Grade level: 3-6

Artifact: A baseball card

Summary: Skeeter learns lessons in confidence and understanding through the game of baseball and through Tommy Scott's dog Pancho.

READING/WRITING CONNECTIONS

1. Read several baseball cards. Discuss the cards, the players pictured, why people collect baseball cards, and the game of baseball.
2. Show the book. Discuss the title and what is happening on the cover.
3. Read the first sentence. Talk about all the information the author provides in that first sentence, such as the assumption that readers would know the correct meaning of *plate* and *outfield*, the nickname of the protagonist, the name of the opposing team, and the inference that Skeeter has a reputation as a hitter since "the men in the outfield stepped back." Discuss the importance of an author knowing his or her audience.
4. Read the first paragraph and discuss the situation facing Skeeter, his feelings, times in life when people might feel the way Skeeter felt at the plate, and times when the students may have experienced similar feelings.
5. Complete first chapter. Brainstorm words that describe Skeeter. Invite predictions about whether Skeeter will be safe or out. Encourage students to provide reasons for their predictions.
6. Distribute a baseball card to each student. Students write about about the person on their card. Share. Display cards with writing on bulletin board.

EXTENSIONS

 VOCABULARY/SPELLING:

plate	outfield	outs	inning	scrub	game
home run	left field	bases	league	clean	double strike
outside	corner	pitcher	cross-handed	hook	southpaw
whiffed	grounded	fly ball	going deep	a single	top of the third
retired	shoestring	catch	struck out	throw-in	double play
fumbled	called time	low pitch	centerfield	home	slow grounder
slide	top of the fifth				

 LIBRARY CONNECTIONS

1. Corpus of work:

Christopher has written many sports classics on basketball, dirt bike racing, football, ice hockey, soccer, track, as well as baseball. Create a display of his baseball books:

❖ *Baseball Pals*
❖ *Catcher with a Glass Arm*
❖ *The Diamond Champs*
❖ *The Fox Steals Home*
❖ *The Kid Who Only Hits Homers*
❖ *Look Who's Playing First Base*
❖ *No Arm in Left Field*
❖ *Shortstop from Tokyo*
❖ *Year Mom Won the Pennant*

2. Learning the Library:

• Show students *Current Biography*, other biographical sources such as the card catalog, almanacs, single-volume reference works, specialized dictionaries, vertical files, and the areas of the library where they can find information on baseball, the history of the game, and the players.

• Discover sources that list baseball cards and their values. Which sources are the best? Students chart the value of a baseball card over time. Can money be made from collecting cards? If so, how?

 ENGLISH/LANGUAGE ARTS CONNECTIONS

1. Listening skills:

Listen to an announcer describing an inning taped from the radio. Watch a video tape of an inning. Discuss.

2. How-to writing:

Divide students into pairs according to their favorite game. They discuss how to play that game. They write a rule book for the game with clear, specific, and concise rules. Display.

3. Subplots:

After the book has been completed, discuss the Pancho, skateboard, falcon, and Idaho subplots.

4. Writing letters:

• While in Idaho, Skeeter writes to Shadow. Write a friendly letter to someone in class.

• Students may become official members of the Matt Christopher Fan Club by writing their request and sending a self-addressed, stamped, business-letter size envelope, to:

Matt Christopher Fan Club
34 Beacon Street
Boston, MA 02108

5. Visiting speaker:

Invite a sports writer or sportcaster to speak to the class about the importance of vivid verbs, precise word choice, and accuracy in writing and speaking. Encourage students to pose questions.

6. Research: Students collect articles, pictures, editorials, feature stories, and ads about baseball to display on the bulletin board.

7. Descriptive writing: Skeeter has a pet falcon, and Tommy has a pet Chihuahua. Both pets are described in the book. Write a description of a pet (real or imaginary). Be sure to give its name.

 ART CONNECTIONS

1. Baseball banners:

Divide students into small groups to make baseball banners. Each group decides on a baseball team (local, state, or national); plans the layout by sketching the idea(s); draws a scaled-down version using graph paper; assembles the banner; and hangs the banner somewhere in the room (or hall).

2. Skateboard fun:

Skeeter's cousin Alan teaches him to skateboard. Make a miniature skateboard: cut a popsicle stick into a two-inch piece, sand and round the rough side to match the other side, color it with markers, cut a straw into two pieces as wide as the popsicle stick, paste the straws onto the popsicle stick to resemble wheels, decorate, and name the skateboard.

3. Invisible dog:

Skeeter and Shadow wished to make Pancho invisible. Make "invisible dogs" by soaking a small dog's collar in white glue and rounding it while wet. Attach a wire to the collar and run the wire through a leash up to about where the hand would hold the leash. Bend it slightly so it curves when you hold the wired leash as if walking a dog.

MATHEMATICS CONNECTIONS

Calculating averages:

Skeeter has a batting average of .714. Write how to figure a baseball player's average for someone who does not know how to calculate baseball averages. Use Skeeter's average as your example.

PHYSICAL EDUCATION CONNECTIONS

Learn the rules of baseball and play a game.

PUBLISHING

GAME DAY! Students share their favorite game or sport. They may bring in what they have written about that game or sport, equipment, books, rules, pictures, videos, or tapes.

The Boxcar Children

Gertrude Chandler Warner

Albert Whitman & Company,
1942,1950,1969,1977

THE BOXCAR CHILDREN
GERTRUDE CHANDLER WARNER

Grade level: 3-5

Artifact: A miniature boxcar or a boxcar made from a box

Summary: Henry, Jessie, Violet, and Benny are orphans who make an old boxcar into a makeshift home. Eventually their grandfather finds them and gives them a real home.

READING/WRITING CONNECTIONS

1. Discuss orphans, the homeless, how people become homeless or orphaned. Invite speculation about how it might feel to be an orphan or without a home. Introduce the word *orphanage*. Discuss orphanages, foster homes, and children's homes.
2. Summarize or read chapters 1 and 2. Read all of chapter 3.
3. Students predict where the children might get the dishes, how they might make four beds, the table, and chairs.
4. Distribute the miniature boxcars, or make the boxcars out of matchbooks turned sideways with tiny buttons glued on as wheels.
5. Students write what they think makes the "Crack, crack, crack!" in the woods. Share.

EXTENSIONS

 VOCABULARY/SPELLING:

Jessie	morning	thunder	blowing	lightning
boxcar	bushes	Henry	Benny	Violet
stump	climbed	shining	waterfall	dishes
engine	track	dinner	pieces	blueberries

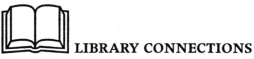 **LIBRARY CONNECTIONS**

1. Corpus of work: Share other books by the author:

   ✤ *Benny Uncovers a Mystery*
   ✤ *Blue Bay Mystery*
   ✤ *Bus Station Mystery*
   ✤ *Caboose Mystery*
   ✤ *The Lighthouse Mystery*
   ✤ *Mike's Mystery*
   ✤ *Mountain Top Mystery*
   ✤ *Mystery Behind the Wall*
   ✤ *Mystery in the Sand*
   ✤ *Mystery Ranch*
   ✤ *Schoolhouse Mystery*
   ✤ *Surprise Island*
   ✤ *The Woodshed Mystery*
   ✤ *The Yellow House Mystery*

2. Related books:

   • Share the Joan Lowery Nixon *Orphans of the Storm* series.
   • Share Eve Bunting's *Fly Away Home*.
   • More mature readers might read Katherine Paterson's *The Great Gilly Hopkins*.
   • Patricia Polacco's sensitive story about a place for unwanted children, *I Can Hear the Sun*.
   • Maurice Sendak's unusual nursery rhymes about homelessness, *We Are All in the Dumps*.

3. Learning the library:

   • Have the librarian show what series books are: named series, author series, and nonfiction subject series, for example. Ask students who are experts on a particular series to participate in a panel discussion about series books. Which are worth reading? Why are series created?

   • Choose a series. Students read different titles in that series. Compare the similarities and differences. How have some series been updated? Are the updates successful?

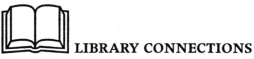 **ENGLISH/LANGUAGE ARTS CONNECTIONS**

1. Summarizing:

Divide students into groups. Give each group 14 index cards (or oaktag paper cut about that size). Each group writes the title and author of the book and their names on the first card. Then they label the remaining thirteen cards by chapter titles. On each card, the group writes a summary of that chapter. Finally students arrange these around the room like so many boxcars, affixing wheels, joining them together with string, and making tracks.

2. Time Sequence:

Distribute long strips of paper. Students construct a time line for the adventures of the boxcar children.

 SOCIAL STUDIES CONNECTIONS

World War II:

Explain that this book was written in 1942 during World War II.

• Speculate how war might orphan children. Discuss what could happen today to orphan children.

• Research displays of patriotism between the year 1941-45. For example: parades, flag displays, leaflet distributions, paper drives, scrape brigades, victory gardens, and United Savings Bonds.

• Research wartime toys. For example: Victory Guns, Victory Painting Sets, Soldier Sailor Sticker Pictures, Wawky-Tawky String Phones, Fighters for Freedom Picture Puzzles, Joe Palooka, and Boy Commandos.

• Research the activities of the Girl Scouts and Boy Scouts.

π MATHEMATICS CONNECTIONS

Problem solving:

• Give students a word problem using the information in the book. Use this example, Jessie bought three loaves of bread. Henry cut one loaf into four pieces, one piece for each of the four children. At one piece a day per child, how many days can the children eat bread?

• Students write their own word problems using the above as a model. Exchange problems. Solve, exchange back, and check.

 HEALTH/ SCIENCE CONNECTIONS

The food groups:

Students make a chart of the four food groups. Chart the foods eaten by the boxcar children. Discuss the nutrition of their meals.

The seasons:

Identify by clues in the book the season of the year and the part of the country where the story takes place. Based on those conclusions, and other information given in the book, students predict what would have happened to the boxcar children if they had not been reunited with their grandfather when they were.

 **ART CONNECTIONS**

Night lights:

Make night lights for the boxcar.

- Use an undented can for the nicest look.
- Remove its label. Scrape or soak off any glue in hot water.
- Draw a pattern on the can with markers.
- Put a rock or piece of wood into the can to brace against. Hammer holes with a nail using the pattern as a guide.
- Carefully place a small candle inside. (Wear a glove so your hand isn't scratched by the jagged edges inside the can.)
- Light the candle and look at the effect of the light and pattern

 PUBLISHING

STORYTELLING IN THE BOXCAR! Darken the classroom. Carefully light the candles in the night lights. Students tell or read a story they have created about the boxcar children.

34

Encyclopedia Brown Boy Detective

Donald J. Sobol

Bantam, 1978,1988

Grade level: 3-5

Artifact: A handbill

Summary: Leroy (Encyclopedia Brown) is a young Sherlock Holmes who solves cases by using his wits. Each chapter presents a different case and challenges the reader to solve the problem too. Solutions are provided in the back of the book.

READING/WRITING CONNECTIONS

1. Discuss detective stories. Talk about specific ones student have read or seen on television. Ask if they ever thought about being a detective.
2. Show a mock-up of the handbill Encyclopedia Brown makes in the book. Talk about it.
3. Read "The Case of Natty Nat." Discuss how Encyclopedia uses what he calls "methods of observation" to solve his cases. Explain that Sherlock Holmes called it "deduction," and Auguste Dupin (Edgar Allan Poe's detective) called it "ratiocination." Challenge students to match wits with Encyclopedia and these great literary detectives.
4. Read "The Case of the Scattered Cards." Divide the class into small groups to discuss the question at the conclusion of the chapter: "How Did Encyclopedia Know?" Have each group write out an answer. Check with the solution given in the book.
5. Make available all sizes and colors of paper. Students choose a piece for a handbill. Display large cards that explain advertising techniques. Talk about each. Ask students if they can connect a technique to some ad they remember from television.
   - Glittering generalities—uses impressive words
   - Emotional appeal—appeals to emotions
   - Testimony—states endorsements by the famous
   - Bandwagon—suggests everybody's doing it
   - Logic—presents sound reasoning
   - Card stacking—gives only one side of the argument

- Name calling—labels to avoid the issue
- Plain folks—attempts to establish a comfort zone.

6. Students design a handbill for their own detective agency using one or more of the advertising techniques discussed. Share and display.

EXTENSIONS

 VOCABULARY/SPELLING:

Encyclopedia	alphabetically	knowledge	criminal
detective	handbills	garage	submarine
kidnapping	blackmail	dirtiest	liar

 LIBRARY CONNECTIONS

1. Corpus of work:

Display other books in this series:
  ✤ *Encyclopedia Brown and the Case of the Midnight Visitor*
  ✤ *Encyclopedia Brown and the Mysterious Handprints*
  ✤ *Encyclopedia Brown and the Case of the Treasure Hunt*
  ✤ *Encyclopedia Brown and the Case of the Disgusting Sneakers*
  ✤ *Encyclopedia Brown/Case of the Secret Pitch*
  ✤ *Encyclopedia Brown Finds the Clue*
  ✤ *Encyclopedia Brown Gets His Man*
  ✤ *Encyclopedia Brown Keeps the Peace*
  ✤ *Encyclopedia Brown Saves the Day*
  ✤ *Encyclopedia Brown Shows the Way*
  ✤ *Encyclopedia Brown Takes the Case*
  ✤ *Encyclopedia Brown Tracks Them Down*

2. Learning the library:
   • Show students how to use the subject catalog to find other detective stories and mystery books.
   • Using reference books, create a chart of ways to collect and interpret evidence to solve crimes.

3. Related book:
   Share George Shannon's *Stories to Solve: Folktales from Around the World* which presents folktales with mysteries to solve.

 ENGLISH/LANGUAGE ARTS CONNECTIONS

1. Slanting a detective story:

Students write a story modeled after *Encyclopedia Brown* in a slant book. They cut the pages for the book at a slant, staple them together, then write the solution upside down on the last page.

2. Writing an interview:

Divide students into pairs. Together they find a story in the newspaper that needs investigation. One student acts as the journalist who interviews his or her partner, who acts as the detective assigned to the case. Each writes up the case from the appropriate point of view.

SOCIAL STUDIES CONNECTIONS

The Civil War:

Encyclopedia Brown solves a case involving a sword from the Civil War. Comb the library to find three interesting facts not mentioned in the chapter about the Civil War, Stonewall Jackson, and the Battle of Bull Run.

π MATHEMATICS CONNECTIONS

1. Problem Solving:

Encyclopedia Brown charges 25 cents per case. At the beginning of the chapter entitled "The Case of the Bank Robber," he counts $3.50 in the treasury of the Brown Detective Agency. If he hasn't spent any money, how many cases has Encyclopedia Brown solved?

2. Problem Posing:

Using money, time, measurement, and distances, compose several word problems involving Encyclopedia Brown, his parents, Sally, Bugs Meany, the Tigers, or other characters in the book.

PUBLISHING

DETECTIVE STORY WRITING ROULETTE! Divide students into groups of four. Each student begins a detective story. They write for about four minutes. Call time. Students pass their papers one place to the right. They take the beginning of the story they were given, read what has been written, and continue it. After about five minutes, call time. Students pass the story one place to the right. They read the first two parts of the story and continue it. After about seven minutes, call time. Students pass the story one place to the right. This time they must conclude the story, tie in the characters, and bring it to a plausible end. Allot sufficient time. Pass the story to the person who wrote the beginning. Share.

35

Dr.
JAC

Tuck Everlasting

Natalie Babbitt

Farrar, Straus and Giroux, 1975

Grade level: 5-12

Artifact: A paper Möbius strip

Summary: The Tuck family drinks from a spring that gives them eternal life. Young Winnie Foster stumbles upon their secret, as does a stranger who wants to market the spring water. The complications that arise make this a timeless tale that operates on many levels.

READING/WRITING CONNECTIONS

1. Divide students into groups of two or three. Using the thesaurus and other resources, each group lists as many synonyms as they can find for the word *everlasting*. Using the dictionary, they check the nuances that distinguish these words one from another. Share lists and discuss.

2. Distribute strips of paper. Students make a Möbius strip, which is one-sided surface. Hold one end of the paper strip in each hand. Give it half a twist, bring the ends together, and fasten. Then they experiment by beginning at one point and drawing a line along the strip. When the line meets its beginning, ask students to connect that result to the book's title. Students make predictions.

3. Read the prologue and chapter 1. Students listen and jot down words or images (implied or explicit) that suggest *everlasting*.

4. Share and discuss as lexical foreshadowings. For example: ferris wheel, the changing seasons, hub of the wheel, wheeling calendar, infinite, earth, axis.

EXTENSIONS

 VOCABULARY/SPELLING:

bubbling	motionless	smeared	curiously	trod
disaster	tangent	ambled	fringes	herd
blurred	widened	tranquil	bovine	axis

contemplation	possessed	dissolved	veer	bough
dimensions	forbidding	gallows	meager	fiery
trespassing	oppressive	mattress	conceal	balmy

 LIBRARY CONNECTIONS

1. Parts of a book:

    Point out the prologue and epilogue. Elicit the purpose of these. Discuss possible reasons why the author would choose these as frames for their stories.

2. Corpus of work by an author:

    Share other books such as:

    ❖ *Goody Hall*

    ❖ *Herbert Rowbarge*

    ❖ *Kneeknock Rise*

    ❖ *Phoebe's Revolt*

3. Find, read, and view other tales about water and life.

 ENGLISH/LANGUAGE ARTS CONNECTIONS

1. Figurative language:

    Two or three groups find examples of similes such as "is going to come apart like wet bread" and metaphors such as "The sun was dropping fast now, a soft red sliding egg yolk..." from assigned chapters. The other groups find symbols such as the music box, the toad, or the spring itself. Discuss why the author would use such figurative language and choose such symbols. Discuss how these enrich the book.

2. Persuasive writing:

    Winnie did not believe in fairy tales. Write a paper persuading Winnie that fairy tales have merit. Share.

3. Inferential thinking:

    In small groups, discuss why Winnie decided never to drink from the spring. Give reasons. Discuss if you agree or disagree with Winnie's decision.

4. Analysis:

    Brainstorm what David Hilbert, a famous German mathematician, meant when he said, "The infinite! No other question has ever moved so profoundly the spirit of man."

 ART CONNECTIONS

1. Drawing descriptions:

    Draw Tuck's "homely little house beside the pond." Use the descriptive passages from chapter 10 as the basis for the drawing.

2. A "Peep" Book:

Draw or paint five different scenes that depict parts of the story, beginning with "the road that led to Treegap." Glue each on a separate 3-X-5-inch piece of oaktag. Make a "peep hole" at an apt place on the first scene and larger "peep holes" on each successive scene. Affix these scenes one behind the other at intervals between two 3-X-13-inch pieces of oaktag that have been folded like an accordion. Pull the card apart, peep into the hole, and view scenes from the book.

π MATHEMATICS CONNECTIONS

The word *infinity* has different meanings in mathematics.

1. The Möbius Strip:

Cut along the line you have drawn on your Möbius strip. Discuss or write what happens. Connect your conclusions to the word *infinity* and to the book

2. Looping:

Use these two looping activities from Marilyn Burns' *Math for Smarty Pants*.

• Start with any number. If even, divide in half. If odd, multiply by three and add one. Keep applying these rules to the resulting answers; do it again and again until you notice the loop's pattern repeating itself.

• Start with any number. Write it as a word. Count its letters. Write that number. Count its letters. Continue until you get four--then you will get four forever.

• Discuss your conclusions. Connect to the word *infinity* and to the book.

3. Research:

Find as much information as you can about the mathematician Georg Cantor who created the symbol to represent the infinite. Find out what you can about Augustus Ferdinand Mobius who discovered the Möbius Strip.

 MUSIC CONNECTIONS

Music plays an important part in the novel. Prepare poems on the animals or insects of the forest using Fleischman's *I Am Phoenix or Joyful Noise: Poems for Two Voices*. Use background music (preferably from a music box). Do the same with the idea of infinity by using Pappas's "The Möbius Strip" from *Math Talk: Mathematical Ideas in Poems for Two Voices*.

 PUBLISHING

Pairs of students present their versions of poems for two voices based on Pappas' work and that of Fleischman, to celebrate EVERLASTING POETRY DAY.

36

Dr. JAC

Taking Sides

Gary Soto

Harcourt, Brace, Jovanovich, 1991

Grade level: 6-8

Artifact: Corn chips

Summary: After moving from the barrio to the suburbs, Lincoln Mendoza finds himself faced with divided loyalties both on and off the basketball court.

READING/WRITING CONNECTIONS

1. Distribute the corn chips. Talk about them as a Hispanic food. Discuss other Hispanic foods such as *chile verde* (green chile stew), *queso* (cheese), *frijoles* (beans), and their assimilation into other American cuisines.
2. Talk about Hispanic words such as *rodeo, mangos, patio,* and *burro* that have also become assimilated into English. Discuss how and why words from one language might become part of another language.
3. Read the first section of chapter 1 (up to the words "from Franklin Junior High to Columbus Junior High).
4. List the Spanish words used: *ese, hombre, menso, vatos*. Discuss their meaning in context. Point out the glossary. Discuss why Soto would use the actual Spanish words, and what that does for the story.
5. Students write about Lincoln's feelings in his new school. Share.

EXTENSIONS

 VOCABULARY/SPELLING:

homeboy	hurled	Flaco	receiver	punk
weird	forearm	muscle	asphalt	handsome
barrio	urban	suburb	ghetto	San Francisco
Sycamore	hovering	dank	ransacked	jackhammers
mulberry tree	splotches	voyage	stomped	

 LIBRARY CONNECTIONS

1. Corpus of work:

Share other works by the author.

❖ *A Summer Life,* a collection of short essays, recreates the images he remembers growing up in Fresno, California.

❖ *Baseball in April and Other Stories,* a collection of short stories, tells of his experiences as a Mexican-American in California's Central Valley.

❖ *Who Will Know Us? New Poems* and *A Fire in My Hands* are poetry books.

2. Research:

Find out what cultural characteristics people bring to this country when they immigrate. How do some of these practices make life in the United States a challenge?

ENGLISH/LANGUAGE ARTS CONNECTIONS

1. **Language study:**

Divide students into teams. Each team:

- Chooses a foreign language
- Finds 10 or more words from that language that have been assimilated into English
- Speculates why those words were assimilated
- Supports that speculation through etymological research
- Shares findings.

2. **Writing dialogue:**

Following Soto's model, students write a brief dialogue incorporating several words or phrases they may know from another language (or they may refer to the glossary in the book for Spanish words and phrases).

3. **Vivid writing:**

Using the section in chapter 12 that describes the second half of the basketball game as a model, students write about a playing a game they know.

4. **Compare/Contrast:**

Draw a Venn Diagram. Label one side section "life in the barrio"; label the other side section "life in the suburbs"; label the center section "what both have in common." As students read the book, they fill in the diagram. Discuss or use for a compare/contrast paper.

5. **Speaking:**

On October 24, 1991, Gary Soto spoke at the Institute of Texan Cultures in San Antonio, Texas. At one point he said, "Things change because you run into teachers who make a difference." Have students talk about teachers who have made a difference in their lives.

SOCIAL STUDIES CONNECTIONS

Research:

1. Early in the book, Lincoln marvels at the Nile because it seems "to oppose gravity by flowing north." Research what Soto means. In small groups, speculate about Lincoln's fascination with Egypt. Talk about why people become fascinated with different topics. Identify topics that intrigue members of the group. Discuss

2. Find out facts about the Sphinx. Based on those facts, write why you think Linc admired it so much. Share.

 MATHEMATICS CONNECTIONS

Problem Solving: (chapter 6)

1. Make a list of the items Linc and Tony see in the thrift store. Create word problems using all or some of these items and their values.

2. Calculate how many soda cans the man pushing the shopping cart would have to collect to go to a movie and have a hamburger and soft drink afterwards. Identify the information you need to solve this problem.

3. How much did Linc and Tony spend (including tax) when they bought gum, sunflower seeds, and a Coke to share? Identify the information you need to solve this problem?

 ART CONNECTIONS

Draw your rendition of the camel driver with the lined face and broken teeth that Linc sees over and over again.

PHYSICAL EDUCATION CONNECTIONS

Gary Soto is an Associate Professor of Chicano Studies at the University of California at Berkeley, but he also volunteers as a karate teacher at a local Boys' Club. Find out what you can about karate. Discuss reasons why Soto would want to teach it.

PUBLISHING

Celebrate the study of Gary Soto during Urban Fiesta Day by viewing his short film *The Bike*. Sample Hispanic foods and discuss what was learned about the Hispanic culture through Soto's writings. Decorate the room with colorful streamers, writing, and research.

37

The Brave

Robert Lipsyte

Harper Collins Children's Books,
1991

Grade level: 8-12

Artifact: A feather stapled to stiff paper or cardboard.

Summary: Alfred Brooks of *The Contender*, now a policeman, collides with Sonny Bear, a 17-year-old heavyweight boxer from the Indian reservation, on the streets of New York City. The result of this collision makes for a powerful and poignant sequel. (Point of information: It is not necessary to have read *The Contender* to understand or appreciate *The Brave*.)

READING/WRITING CONNECTIONS

1. Show the book's dust jacket. Speculate about possible meanings of the title, the symbols of the hawk, the boxing gloves, the young man's expression, and the colors.
2. Write the words *monster* and *bad spirit* on the board, overhead, or chart. Ask students to keep those words in mind as you read chapter 1.
3. After the reading, students fold a paper in half and write the words *monster* on one side and *bad spirit* on the other. Invite them to quickly write what they associated with those words. Discuss.
4. Read the section in chapter 13 that begins, "'You know what a contender is?'" and ends, "'You learn to do that, you can beat anything, anywhere.'" Talk about that section in relation to chapter 1. Speculate and predict.
5. Distribute the feather/papers. Tell students to think of their feathers as symbols for the Hawk. As they listen to (or read) the book they are to jot down their thoughts about this symbol on the paper. Explain that their ideas may change as the story progresses. Encourage them to be honest in order to see what emerges.

EXTENSIONS

 VOCABULARY/SPELLING:

swaggered	aisle	hillbilly	bozos	tommyhawk
massaged	biceps	fluorescent	Moscondaga	reservation
beckoned	referee	gouging	swigged	nostril
staggered	snagged	snickered	neutral	cantaloupe
disqualification	uppercut	capsule	accidental	sidestepped
backpedaled	spiky	cornermen	hoisted	hurtling

 LIBRARY CONNECTIONS

1. Corpus of work:

   Share other works by the author:

   ❖ *Free to Be Muhammad Ali*

   ❖ *Assignment: Sports*

   ❖ *The Contender*

   ❖ *Jock and Jill*

   ❖ *One Fat Summer*

   ❖ *Summer Rules*

   ❖ *The Summerboy*

2. Through library reference books, interviews, and research, students discover how sports statistics are compiled and published. Start with high school sports and then investigate professional sports. What are the best and most accurate sources of information?

 ENGLISH/LANGUAGE ARTS CONNECTIONS

1. **Slang dictionary:**

   Compile a slang dictionary of words and terms you know. Use Stick's slang and Doll's translations for ideas.

2. **Word and string games:**

   Create a word game or a string game that Jake might have used with Sonny. Write the rules and directions. Play your game with a classmate.

3. **Writing folk or fairy tales:**

   Throughout the book, Sonny accuses Jake of telling fairy tales. Write the legend in the book as Jake believes it.

4. **Viewing/Speaking:**

   Watch one of Muhammad Ali's fights on video. Talk about it the way you think Jake and Sonny did.

5. **Film reviews:**

   Watch *American Ninja* or *Karate Kid* on video. Write a film review.

6. **Predicting:**

   Brooks was a fighter. Write or talk about what will happen to him if Lipsyte writes a third book in this series.

7. **Figurative language:**

   Words such as *mushrooms* and *mules* have double meanings in the book, as do phrases such as "the selling of death to kids." Talk about those meanings. Find examples of other figurative language.

8. **Character sketches:**

   Choose a character: Sonny, his mother, Jake, Brooks, Stick, Doll, Glen Hoffer, or Martin. Write a character sketch.

 SOCIAL STUDIES CONNECTIONS

Research:

- Look up information on the Gotham Gloves, the Golden Gloves and boxing in the Olympics. Share findings with the class.
- Find biographies of Joe Lewis and Muhammad Ali. Compare them to contemporary boxers.

 ART CONNECTIONS

Interpretation:

Sonny took his sketchbook, pencils, and charcoals with him when he left the reservation. Draw birds, leaves, or Running Braves as you think Sonny drew them. Share. Talk about your interpretations.

Prediction:

Draw what you think Sonny would draw after living in the city. Discuss.

 PHYSICAL EDUCATION CONNECTIONS

Practice of skills:

Jack worked on Sonny's balance, footwork, and concentration through games. In pairs, work on the stick kick and the hand clap. Keep a log of your progress. Try other partners.

MUSIC CONNECTIONS

Listening:

1. Sonny begins to listen to the music of *Grateful Dead* on the bus. Play some of their music and discuss.

2. Jake uses the animal alphabet to hone Sonny's listening skills. Create an animal alphabet of your own. Do it to rap for a group or for the class. Check which animal(s) they didn't hear.

3. Create other alphabet games using inanimate objects, people's names, colors, and so forth.

 PUBLISHING

Sit in a square formation as if sitting around a BOXING RING. Share the feather/papers.

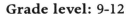

I Am the Cheese

Robert Cormier

Pantheon Books, 1977

Grade level: 9-12

Artifact: A piece of cheese.

Summary: Adam begins a search for his father and the truth of his own past. As he makes this journey, the reader progresses through many levels of meaning concerning Adam, his family, and today's society.

READING/WRITING CONNECTIONS

1. Distribute small pieces of cheese. Have students speculate on the significance of cheese in the title. If students do not suggest cheese as the bait in a trap or "the cheese stands alone," as in "The Farmer in the Dell," guide them to those possibilities.
2. Explain that Cormier did not number his book's chapters. As they listen to or read the first five chapters, ask them to speculate on why he omitted chapter numbers. Brainstorm things they notice in the alternating chapters.
3. Reevaluate and discuss earlier predictions.

EXTENSIONS

 VOCABULARY/SPELLING:

pedaling	furiously	handlebars	slithering	oozes
accelerates	suspicion	licenses	raucously	squints
suffocation	immensity	aluminum	philosophically	vista
momentum	tentatively	panicky	sulphur	aura

 **LIBRARY CONNECTIONS**

1. Corpus of work:

    Display other books by author.

    ❖ *After the First Death*

    ❖ *Beyond the Chocolate War*

    ❖ *The Bumblebee Flies Anyway*

    ❖ *The Chocolate War*

    ❖ *Fade*

    ❖ *Other Bells for Us to Ring*

    ❖ *Tenderness*

    ❖ *We All Fall Down*

2. Related books:

    ❖ Share books that contain the classic children's song.

    ❖ Kathy Parkinson's *The Farmer in the Dell*

    ❖ Mary M. Rae's *The Farmer in the Dell: A Singing Game*

    ❖ Diane Zuromski's (Illustrator) *The Farmer in the Dell*

3. Have the librarian join the teacher in a discussion of Cormier's books. Explore his use of multiple layers of meaning and lack of plot resolution. Ask students to speculate on Cormier's use of current events to inspire intense drama.

 ENGLISH/LANGUAGE ARTS CONNECTIONS

1. **Allusions:**

    • Introduce literary allusions through the book's title. Divide students into small groups. Each group researches *The Web and the Rock* by Thomas Wolfe, speculates why Cormier used it so early in the novel, why he used it instead of the better-known sequel *You Can't Go Home Again,* and why later in the novel Cormier distinguishes Thomas Wolfe from Tom Wolfe.

    • Point out Cormier's use of "Rotary Club," "VW," "Red Sox," "Patriots," and "A & P" to introduce cultural allusions. Working in groups, students list other cultural allusions in the book. Write how they would explain these to Anglo-Saxons, Victorians, Puritans, or people living during the Renaissance.

    • Explain "Hertz" as a cultural and a personal allusion for Adam. Students write example of such allusions and elaborate on origins. Share.

2. **Symbolism:**

    Review the symbols of cheese in "Farmer in the Dell" and as bait in a mousetrap. Students find and discuss other examples of symbolism in the novel. Share and explain the meaning of each symbol.

3. **Levels of meaning:**

    Use Cormier's novel to introduce William Faulkner. Connect to his use of the literary device "multiple levels of consciousness." Cull examples from *As I Lay Dying, The Sound and the Fury,* or *Absalom, Absalom!*

4. **Novel/Video:**

Watch the video *I Am the Cheese* (available at Blockbuster Video). In groups, list similarities and differences between the book and film. Discuss or use as prewriting for a paper.

5. **Word Study:**

Look up the word *dell.* Connect its meaning to the story.

 ART CONNECTIONS

1. **Interpretations:**

Study the dust jacket. The cover is from Robert Vickrey's painting *"Corner Seat."* Discuss why this painting was chosen. Agree or disagree with the choice. Find other paintings that would serve equally well as a cover. Justify your choices.

2. **Collage:**

Collage art juxtaposes images to create meaning much the way Cormier juxtaposes chapters to create meaning. Students create a collage that matches the book.

3. **Analysis:**

Several versions of the cover for the book have been published since 1977. Find the various dust jackets and compare them. Discuss the artists interpretations.

 **SOCIAL STUDIES CONNECTIONS**

1. **Map work:**

Trace Adam's route as he thinks it on a road map of the Massachusetts and Vermont area. Draw a map of the real route Adam took.

2. **Research:**

Find information on the United States Department of Re-Identification or the government's witness relocation and protection policies. Consider this information as compared to the information woven into the novel and draw conclusions. Share.

π**MATHEMATICS CONNECTIONS**

Estimating:

Discuss making an estimate. Adam estimates he can make 10 miles an hour on his bike. The old man figures Adam can make four or five. Discuss the difference in the two estimates and why they are so different.

PHYSICAL EDUCATION CONNECTIONS

1. Research:

   Find information on the biking and the physical conditioning biking takes. Project that information for Adam. Take into consideration the medication he may have been taking and his psychological condition.

2. Kick the Can:

   Play "Kick the Can," a game referenced in the novel.

3. Drug Awareness:

   Find information on the types of drugs that are beneficial to people with certain conditions. Then project how beneficial drugs can be abused.

 PUBLISHING

Students, working in pairs or in small groups, prepare a TEXT RENDERING or an interpretation of the final chapter. They may repeat words, phrases, sentences. They may echo, chorus, rap. They may omit words, rearrange words, but they may not add words. Groups present their text rendering to the class.

39

Maniac Magee

Jerry Spinelli

Little, Brown and Company, 1990.
Newbery Medal and the Boston Globe-Horn Book Award for fiction

Grade level: 6-12

Artifact: A sneaker shoelace

Summary: After his parents' death, Jeffrey Lionel Magee becomes a legend because of his athletic accomplishments. He also helps kids from both the East and West Side see through new eyes.

READING/WRITING CONNECTIONS

1. Distribute a copy of the chant the grade-school girls say as they jump rope. Everyone reads the chant silently, then they recite it the way they think the girls said it as they jumped rope.
2. Discuss what the chant says. Lead students to see how this could be a tall tale or a legend. Talk about the origins of tall tales and legends.
3. Read the prologue "Before the Story." Extend the discussion on tall tales and legends by asking students what Spinelli could mean by "and be very, very careful not to let the facts get mixed up with the truth."
4. Students tear three pieces of paper in half. They number them 1 to 6.
5. Explain that you will read the first five chapters of the book. After each chapter they write their reaction the half sheets of paper. On paper six they write what they think will happen next. As they are writing their predictions, give each student a sneaker shoelace. Share predictions in small groups.

EXTENSIONS

 VOCABULARY/SPELLING:

cockroach	maniac	legacy	monument
trolley	motorman	kaboodle	musicale
auditorium	bulging	smatter	giggling
lunging	scraggly	puzzlement	encyclopedia

whirled	mitts	spiraling	commotion
matinees	occasionally	shuffling	wretch
boomerangs	zillion	paralyzed	yawning
maw	python	hallucination	emanations

 LIBRARY CONNECTIONS

1. Corpus of work:

Share other works by the same author:

❖ *Dump Days*

❖ *Jason and Marceline*

❖ *Night of the Whale*

❖ *Space Station Seventh Grade*

❖ *Who Put That Hair in My Toothbrush?*

2. Parts of a book:

Teach the function of the prologue. Discuss how books are divided into chapters and parts and how the informational footnotes are used.

3. Areas of the library:

• Find books that are good read-alouds. How do you choose these books? Practice reading aloud to younger students. What are the best techniques?

• Students prepare an annotated bibliography of other books about the homeless directed toward children or teenagers. Have them booktalk this list to its intended audience.

• Maniac buys books for five or ten cents inside the door of the library. Assign groups of students a stack in the library. They decide what books in that stack are eligible to be put on sale. Discuss criteria for their decisions.

 ENGLISH/LANGUAGE ARTS CONNECTIONS

1. **Figurative language:**

• Draw pictures that depict the literal meaning of the following the figurative expressions:

"His stomach was a cereal box"

"His heart a sofa spring"

"Soles of both sneakers hanging by their hinges and flopping open like dog tongues"

"The book came flapping like a wounded duck and fell at Jeffrey's feet."

• Find other similes and metaphors in the novel.

2. **Research:**

Find the name of the musical that contained the song "Talk to the Animals" (*Dr. Doolittle*). Record the source.

3. **Letter writing:**
   Mrs. Beale becomes upset when she hears Maniac talking trash. Write a letter of apology from Maniac to Mrs. Beale.
4. **Story writing:**
   Maniac tells Grayson, "Everybody has a story." Write your story.
5. **Children's books:**
   To help Grayson read, they buy 20 old picture books such as *The Story of Babar, Mike Mulligan's Steam Shovel*, and *The Little Engine That Could*. Visit the children's section of the library. Make a list of the other 17 you think they bought. Explain why you chose those books.

 SOCIAL STUDIES CONNECTIONS

The atlas:
Maniac Magee was born in Bridgeport. At least eleven states have a town named Bridgeport.

• Consult an atlas to record the names of those states.
• Using the information given in chapter 1 and in the atlas, decide in which state Maniac was born. Be prepared to defend your conclusion.

 MATHEMATICS CONNECTIONS

1. **Proofs:**
   The story goes that Maniac "absolutely, dead-center proved" to Grayson using an old geometry book, that the two legs on an isosceles triangle are equal. Write out that proof.
2. **Designing:**
   Design and draw "the pillbox," as George, John, and the Cobras called it. Give the dimensions.

 ART CONNECTIONS

Draw one of Maniac Magee's sneakers. Put the artifact shoelace into the sketch.

PUBLISHING

Display Spinelli's books, all the student writing and research, and students' art. Call the display WRITING AND READING ON A SHOESTRING.

40 *Dragonwings*

Laurence Yep

Harper & Row Publishers, 1975
Newbery Honor Book

Grade level: 7-12

Artifact: A small tissue-paper kite

Summary: Moon Shadow comes to America from China. Through him readers experience life in San Francisco during the early twentieth century. Yep considers this book a historical fantasy.

READING/WRITING CONNECTIONS

1. Distribute pieces of colored tissue paper. Cut out a kite shape and paste it on a large piece of stiff white paper. Add string or ribbon for the kite's tail.
2. Read the "kite" section in chapter 1, "The Land of the Demons (February-March, 1903")" that begins, "To tell the truth" and ends, "scoop the gold into big buckets." Caution students to listen carefully as you read.
3. Explain that kites were thought to have originated in China about 3,000 years ago. Discuss how interest in kites and flying kites may be a manifestation of a interest in flying. Extend the discussion by explaining that Yep wrote this book after reading a newspaper account of Fung Joe Guey, who attempted to fly a biplane he designed in Oakland in 1909.

EXTENSIONS

 VOCABULARY/SPELLING:

heirlooms	leash	phoenix	nuisance	palace
demon	reckoning	swallow	soared	flick
caterpillar	mountain	thousand	buckets	scoop

 LIBRARY CONNECTIONS

1. Corpus of work:
   Share other works by the author:
   - ❖ *Child of the Owl*
   - ❖ *Dragon of the Lost Sea*
   - ❖ *Kind Hearts & Gentle Monsters*
   - ❖ *The Mark Twain Murders*
   - ❖ *Mountain Light*
   - ❖ *The Rainbow People*
   - ❖ *Dragon Steel*
   - ❖ *The Serpent's Children*
   - ❖ *Sweetwater*

2. Share *City Kids in China* by Peggy Thomson. Students compare the photographs of the Chinese city of Changsha with photographs of their own community. Discuss the adjustment faced when one moves to a new community. Use library resources to compare populations of cities in China to those in the United States. Is any American city similar to Changsha in population, density, and so forth?

3. Related books:
   - ❖ Jean Fritz's *Homesick:My Own Story* tells of Fritz's childhood in China.
   - ❖ Arthur Bowie Chrisman's *Shen of the Sea: Chinese Stories for Children* (Newbery Medal) presents a series of fascinating Chinese stories.
   - ❖ Elizabeth Foreman Lewis's *Young Fu of the Upper Yangtze*(Newbery Medal) tells of the turmoil of life in China during the 1920's.
   - ❖ Patricia C. Wrede's chapter from "The Enchanted Forest Chronicles" *Dealing with Dragons* and *Searching for Dragons* presents good dragons and wicked wizards.
   - ❖ Lee J. Hindle's *Dragon Fall*, winner of the Flare Competition depicts the monsters of Gabe's imagination.
   - ❖ Margaret Leaf's *Eyes of the Dragon* tells the story of painting dragon's eyes.
   - ❖ Eric Carle's *Dragons Dragons & Other Creatures That Never Were* is an illustrated compilation of poems about dragons and other creatures by different authors.
   - ❖ Hosie and Leonard Baskin's *A Book of Dragons* features twenty-two dragons representing many cultures.

ENGLISH/LANGUAGE ARTS CONNECTIONS

1. **Letter writing:**
   Assume the persona of Moon Shadow's mother. Write a letter to Moon Shadow. Assume the persona of Moon Shadow. Write a letter to Grandmother.

2. **Imagery:**
   Divide students into groups. As a group, read chapter 3 "The Dragon Man (April,

1903)." Cull images from that chapter to categorize as: visual, aural, olfactory, kinetic, or images that affect the sense of taste.

3. **Symbolism:**

Names such as Old Deerfoot, Hand Clap, Uncle Bright Star, Moon Shadow, Black Dog, and Windrider are symbolic. Find other symbolic names in the novel. Create symbolic names for yourself and others you know. Explain the symbolism.

4. **Dragons in literature:**

Mrs. Whitlaw talks about wicked dragons and how St. George killed many of them. Moon Shadow is horrified because the Chinese dragon Shen Lung brings good luck. Research dragons in literature.

 SOCIAL STUDIES CONNECTIONS

Map Study:

- On a map of China, find the Canton province. Find the Fragrant Mountains. Research where these Chinese from Canton immigrated.
- Find the mountains and describes the event that caused the Chinese immigrants to call America the Land of the Gold Mountain.

Research:

Divide students into five research groups:

Group One investigates the beginnings of "Chinatowns" in America.

Group Two lists common Chinese names and their meanings.

Group Three researches the T'ang Dynasty rulers of China from 618-907 A.D.

Group Four finds information about the Chinese Exclusion Act of 1882.

Group Five records facts and statistics about the California earthquake mentioned in the book.

 SCIENCE CONNECTIONS

Wind and weather:

Experiment with kites under various weather conditions. Keep a log of what you learn. (Obviously, kite flying during lightening storms is *not* recommended!)

Stereoptical images:

Show students a stereopticon. Explain how it works. Read about Moon Shadow's experience with it in chapter 6 "The Demoness (May, 1905)." Discuss.

 PHYSICAL EDUCATION CONNECTIONS

Play the game "Jackstraws" the way it is described in chapter 9 "The Dragon Wakes (December, 1905-April, 1906)."

ART CONNECTIONS

Garbage bag kites: Follow Susan Milord's detailed instructions in *Adventures in Art* to make plastic bag kites. She also gives kite-flying tips.

 PUBLISHING

Create a bulletin board OUR DRAGONWINGS! Use colored tissue paper and pastels or colored chalk to create the illusions of a dragons. Display students' drawings, kites, writing, and research. Make books part of the display.

41

Dr. JAC

Sadako and the Thousand Paper Cranes

Eleanor Coerr

Dell Publishing, 1977

Grade level: 4-7

Artifact: An origami paper crane

Summary: This poignant story of a girl who lived in Hiroshima when the United States dropped the atom bomb and who died of leukemia as a result of radiation from that bomb.

READING/WRITING CONNECTIONS

1. Hold a gold origami paper crane in your hand as you talk about the crane and its mythology and symbolism in Japanese culture. Explain that the golden crane is important on many levels in this book.
2. Show the book's cover. Invite predictions about the book.
3. Approach the reading of this book in one of two ways. Either read it in its entirety in two or three days, or read the prologue, followed by an excerpt from each chapter, and the epilogue.
4. Invite students to write down problems. Share. Discuss tangible objects that could possibly solve or ease those problems, such as putting a pinwheel on a bike to remind a consistently late student that time is passing.
5. Discuss how having or doing something concrete can often help a problem. Connect to Sadako's making the origami cranes.

EXTENSIONS

 VOCABULARY/SPELLING:

memorial	leukemia	radiation	transfusion
ceremonies	prickled	scarred	Buddhist
bamboo	kimono	amidst	rustle
x-rayed	plumped	lopsided	parasols

 **LIBRARY CONNECTIONS**

1. Corpus of work:

   Explain that Eleanor Coerr lived in Japan. She read Sadako's letters and talked to many people who knew her. Share Coerr's other books:

   ❖ *The Big Balloon Race*
   ❖ *Chang's Paper Pony*
   ❖ *The Josefina Story Quilt*
   ❖ *Lady with a Torch*

2. Related books:

   • Read Junko Morimoto's *My Hiroshima,* in which she recounts her memories of Hiroshima before and after the war.

   • Read Yukio Tsuchiya's *Faithful Elephants: A True Story of Animals, People and War,* which tells how three elephants in a Tokyo zoo were put to death because of the war. Their monument, like Sadako's, is continuously decorated with *senba-tsuru,* thousands of paper cranes made by children.

   • Read other books about cranes, such as Anne Laurin's *Perfect Crane,* Sumiko Yagawa's *The Crane Wife,* and Allen Say's *The Tree of Cranes.*

3. Learning the library:

   Find a detailed map of Hiroshima, Japan, and the damage caused by the atomic bomb explosion. Compare this to a map of Hiroshima before the bombing and to a map of Japan today. Why were the bombs dropped on Hiroshima and Nagasaki? Why have nuclear weapons not been used since?

 ART CONNECTIONS

1. Origami:

   Fold origami paper cranes. Use Florence Sakade's *Origami, Japanese Paper Folding* for directions. Hang these by threads as *senba-tsuru.*

2. Interpretative drawing:

   Draw renditions of Sadako's monument in Hiroshima Peace Park.

3. Making a miniature doll:

   Make miniature *Kokeshi* dolls like the one Sadako's classmates brought her. Use wooden tongue depressors and dress in kimonos.

4. Creating designs:

   Using a long sheet of colored butcher paper, create designs for your own *tatami* mat.

 **SOCIAL STUDIES CONNECTIONS**

1. Facts about Hiroshima:

   Working in groups, find facts about Hiroshima. Write these on butcher paper and display for all to read.

2. Making maps:

Construct a map of Japan. Label Hiroshima, Nagasaki, and the capital, Tokyo.

 SCIENCE CONNECTIONS

1. Research the disease leukemia:

Write a report in which you identify the disease, describe the symptoms, give the causes, and discuss possible cures.

2. Research nuclear radioactivity:

Research natural radioactivity in radium and uranium. Find information about alpha particles, beta particles, and gamma radiation, isotopes uranium-235, and plutonium-239.

3. Research the "Manhattan Project."

Find out things such as what it did, who was involved in it, and where it was located.

ENGLISH/LANGUAGE ARTS CONNECTIONS

1. Collaborative writing:

Working in pairs, list things about Japan before and after World War II. Write a collaborative paper entitled "The Two Japans."

2. Writing poems:

Working in pairs, write poems using the Japanese form of haiku and tankas.

3. Writing stories:

Chizuko told Sadako the old story of the crane. After hearing Sadako's story, students add to Chizuko's version by writing their own version.

4. Writing letters:

Sadako wrote letters to friends and pen pals. Write a letter to a friend or pen pal. Tell about Sadako.

Write letters to: National Association for the Education of Young Children, 1834 Connecticut Ave., N.W.,Washington, DC 20009. Ask for information on helping young children understand the worldwide threat of war and nuclear arms and ways to seek peaceful solutions.

5. Playing with language:

When Sadako had visitors, they played games, shared riddles, and sang songs. Working in a group create a game, some riddles, or some songs you would share if you visited Sadako.

PHYSICAL EDUCATION CONNECTIONS

Sadako was a runner. List the names of different races or different kinds of races. Practice some.

PUBLISHING

CELEBRATE PEACE DAY! Prepare *furoshiki* bundles of egg rolls, chicken and rice, pickled plums, radishes, and bean cakes. Roll out the *tatami mats,* sit on them and discuss all the things learned during this study, using the opportunity to display projects and writings.

The
Best
of
Books
for
Special
Days

Happy Birthday, Ronald Morgan!

Patricia Reilly Giff

Puffin Books, 1986

Birthdays

Artifact: A gold paper crown

Summary: Ronald has two problems: no school birthday and no best friend. It turns out that he is in for a surprise on both counts.

READING/WRITING CONNECTIONS

1. Show the cover. Invite students to make predictions about why Ronald Morgan looks the way he does. Ask students to identify the musical instrument on the dedication page. Discuss the illustration on the title page. Speculate on the time of year and how that might affect Ronald Morgan's birthday.
2. Read the story. Discuss birthdays in general, what happens and why. Discuss feelings about birthdays. At appropriate times throughout the book, ask students how Ronald Morgan feels. Ask them to give reasons for their answers.
3. Ask how many students celebrate their birthdays during a school vacation. Explain that since some people have birthdays during school, whereas others have birthdays during school vacations, the class will participate in a birthday celebration for everyone.
4. Distribute gold paper and help students cut out crowns with points, like the one Miss Tyler made. They wear their crowns as they draw and write a birthday card for someone in the class. (Draw names out of a hat.) Share.

EXTENSIONS

 VOCABULARY/SPELLING:

tambourine	knuckles	frowned	birthday	Thursday
sneakers	swallowed	present	puppy	private
personal	three-legged race	chocolate	delicious	icing

LIBRARY CONNECTIONS

1. When Ronald Morgan's class goes to the library, they tell stories. Invite students to tell stories about a birthday they remember or about some birthday they wish they had had. Share books that explore birthday observations in various cultures.

2. After the stories, Ronald Morgan visits the Quiet Corner. Show students how to locate the quiet area in the library. Talk about the purpose of the quiet area. Show students other sections of the library. Explain the purposes of those sections. Discuss proper behavior in the quiet area and in other sections of the library.

 INTEGRATED ACTIVITY

Have students make tambourines using Margaret McLean's *Make Your Own Musical Instruments* (pp. 12-13) for step-by-step directions. Practice singing and playing the tambourines as preparation for accompaniment of a rendition of "Happy Birthday."

 PUBLISHING

Display birthday cards on a HAPPY BIRTHDAY TO EVERYONE! bulletin board. Decorate the room with crêpe paper streamers. Students sing and play "Happy Birthday." If possible celebrate with lemon cookies and orange juice.

Agatha's Feather Bed: Not Just Another Wild Goose Story

Carmen Agra Deedy

Peachtree, 1991

Common Sense Day
January 29

Artifact: A feather

Summary: Agatha uses common sense when six angry geese come to reclaim their feathers.

READING/WRITING CONNECTIONS

1. Distribute feathers. Divide students into groups. Assign a scribe. Ask students to list as many purposes for feathers as they can. Share.
2. Show the cover of the book. Explain to students that although this story tells about common sense, it does other things too. Ask students to listen for idioms and to look closely at the items pictured in the borders.
3. Read the story. Stop for predictions at appropriate places.
4. Brainstorm as many puns, idioms, and word plays as students remember. Reread to check.
5. Write the poem Agatha tells all her customers on a chart. (Use later on bulletin board.) Invite students to recite it with you. Discuss its common sense. Discuss how Agatha uses common sense to solve her problem. Elicit a working definition for *common sense*.

EXTENSIONS

VOCABULARY/SPELLING:

sandwiched	skyscrapers	Manhattan	fabric	cotton boll	ducky
linen	flax	catalog	tortoiseshell	flossed	swirls
mattress	boar-bristle	shivering	gaggle	quacks	plucky
scissors	fleecy	extremely	grateful	magnificent	gander

LIBRARY CONNECTIONS

Extend the idioms in the book by challenging students to research the meaning of the following list of idioms and write a common-sense sequel to Agatha's story using some or all of them.

a sitting duck	a lame duck	a dead duck	like water off a duck's back
say boo to a goose	goose step	swan song	all your geese are swans
proud as a peacock	wise as an owl	eagle eye	to take like a duck to water
feather in one's cap	featherweight	bird-eye view	make the feathers fly
in fine feathers		Mother Goose	smooth ruffled feathers

to feather one's own nest
the early bird catches the worm

birds of a feather flock together
to kill two birds with one stone

 INTEGRATED ACTIVITY

1. Divide students into pairs. As partners they generate a list of questions about something mentioned in the book, for example "boar-bristle brush." They decide on three good questions from their lists, which they exchange with another pair.
2. The second pair researches that item and then writes out the answers to the questions they were given.

 PUBLISHING

Display answers around Agatha's poem. Title it EVERYTHING COMES FROM SOMETHING!

44

Somebody Loves You, Mr. Hatch

Eileen Spinelli

Bradbury Press, 1991

February 14: Valentine's Day

Artifact: A replica of an antique valentine

Summary: Reclusive Mr. Hatch receives an anonymous valentine, which changes his life. Realizing it was delivered to him by mistake, Mr. Hatch begins to resume his old ways, but his neighbors and friends have other ideas.

READING/WRITING CONNECTIONS

1. Write "Somebody loves you." on board or chart. Brainstorm the feelings that sentence evokes. Ask students how they would feel if they received an anonymous valentine. Discuss.
2. Introduce the book by explaining this is what happened to Mr. Hatch.
3. After the story, divide students into small groups. Each group lists names of specific people who would not expect to receive a valentine from them, such as the lady in the cafeteria, a senior citizen who lives down the street, a distant cousin. Students circle one person they might surprise with a valentine card.
4. Students replicate antique cards by using paper doilies in silver, white, and gold, as well as ribbons and dried flowers. Their cards may open like fans, pop up, or have moveable flaps.

EXTENSIONS

 VOCABULARY/SPELLING:

shoelace	factory	mustard	sandwich	newsstand
aftershave	cafeteria	chocolates	magazine	Valentine's Day
mysterious	platefuls	pitcher	picnic	harmonica
uneasy	fetched	heart-shaped		

LIBRARY CONNECTIONS

1. Show students how to locate addresses in a telephone book. Demonstrate how to alphabetize to the second and third letter. Show students how to locate the ZIP code.
2. Practice addressing envelopes.

 INTEGRATED ACTIVITY

1. Distribute five three-inch hearts: one red, two purple, and two pink.
2. Read the following word problem. (this may be reworded to fit different grade levels.) "Maria wanted to see if Jesse could build a heart totem pole using five hearts and five clues. Jesse did. Can you? Here are the clues: a. No hearts of the same color are next to each other. b. The top heart is not pink. c. The heart in the center is not red. d. One pink heart is just below a red one. e. The bottom heart is not pink."
3. Work this problem on the overhead along with students. Divide students into small groups. Distribute several white hearts to each group. Each group formulates a design, using the hearts, decides on metaphoric language for that design (e.g., "moon-shaped" instead of "round"), and writes clues for others to try to recreate the design.
4. Exchange clues. Groups work out the designs according to the clues. Check.
5. Discuss what was learned from this activity.

 PUBLISHING

Affix designs and clues on cardboard for a HEARTS TO YOU! bulletin board display.

45

Arthur's April Fool

Marc Brown

Little, Brown and Company, 1983

April 1: April Fool's Day

Artifact: A cardboard tube telescope

Summary: Binky threatens to ruin Arthur's tricks at the April Fool's Day assembly, but Arthur outsmarts him.

READING/WRITING CONNECTIONS

1. Talk about April Fool's Day and the meaning of the word *fool*. Elicit from students the kinds of tricks and pranks people play on this day. Explain that this is an old custom dating back to when April 1 marked the end of an eight-day New Year's celebration. Some people kept that custom even after the calendar was changed and January 1st marked the New Year, so these people were called April's fools.
2. Show the cover of the book. Discuss what Arthur might be doing. Ask students to identify the clues that led them to their answers.
3. Talk about each of Arthur's friends pictured at the book's beginning. Ask the students to tell what is funny about each picture.
4. Read the book. This book lends itself to frequent discussion of sequence and predictions.
5. Give students two cardboard tubes, one shorter than the other. Students insert one into the other to resemble a telescope. They tape clear food wrap or contact paper over the ends. They paint and decorate their telescopes. Then they write what they see through their telescopes. Share.

EXTENSIONS

 VOCABULARY/SPELLING:

sneezing	fake	telescope	threatening	practicing
favorite	Godzilla	pulverize	cheeseburger	nightmares
principal	auditorium	volunteer	pipsqueak	whispered
secret	twerp	shadow	assembly	screamed

LIBRARY CONNECTIONS

1. Share and display a corpus of work by the author. See Sharron L. McElmeel's *Bookpeople: A First Album* for a selected bibliography and a brief biography.
2. Share books on magic tricks and practice execution of some.
3. Students choose their favorite Brown book and do a book talk.

 INTEGRATED ACTIVITY

1. Make a class *April Fool's Animal Alphabet Book*. Create the first page together with students so they can use it for a model. Because Arthur is an aardvark, begin with Aardvark.
2. Let students create other pages individually or in small groups. They write the name of the animal, use words starting with the same letter to describe the animal, include facts about the animal, draw the animal, and add anything else. The April Fool's trick is to hide something extra on the page for the reader to find. Students provide an answer key for the back of the book.

 **PUBLISHING**

Hold a FIND WHAT'S HIDDEN HUDDLE. Students form a group huddle, exchange animal alphabet pages, and search for the hidden extras. Bind and display the finished alphabet book.

46

*Wilfrid Gordon
McDonald Partridge*

Mem Fox

Kane/Miller Book Publishers, 1985

Wilfrid Gordon McDonald Partridge
Written by Mem Fox   Illustrated by Julie Vivas

May is Senior Citizen Month

Artifact: A memory book

Summary: Wilfrid discovers the meaning of memory as he helps Miss Nancy find hers.

READING/WRITING CONNECTIONS

1. Show the two-page title spread and invite commentary. Discuss senior citizens, the elderly, and older people the students may know. Ask if anyone has visited a senior citizen facility or an old-age or nursing home. Discuss.
2. Before reading the book, speculate on the joys and the problems of being a senior citizen.
3. Read the book.
4. Distribute paper. Students fold into an eight-page book.
   - Fold a large piece of paper in half, short end to short end, and crease.
   - Fold one side back halfway and crease; fold the other side back halfway and crease.
   - Keeping the paper folded, fold it short end to short end and crease.
   - Unfold the last fold and allow sides to flip down (looks like a tent).
   - Rip or cut carefully down from the peak of the tent, where the center folds meet. Rip or cut only to next fold.
   - Pick the paper up with one hand on either side of the cut. Fold down so the cut is across the top. Recrease the one fold.
   - Fold into the shape of a book.
5. After writing the title on the front cover and writing "About the Author" on the back cover, students label the pages: Warm Memories, Memories From Long Ago, Sad Memories, Funny Memories, Precious Memories, and Recent Memories.
6. Students write one memory on one of the appropriate pages. Share. (Students may add to their books throughout the month.)

EXTENSIONS

 VOCABULARY/SPELLING:

cricket   tram   precious   speckled   button-up boots   porridge

 LIBRARY CONNECTIONS

1. Invite several senior citizens to talk to the students or to read or tell a story. Ask guest speakers to share their memories of libraries and their importance.
2. Prepare a basket of memories. Help students do what Wilfrid did, that is, make their memories concrete by finding things to represent them. Add to the basket daily. Invite one student each day to tell about his or her memory. Display the memory basket by the checkout desk for students to enjoy while checking out books.

 INTEGRATED ACTIVITY

1. Interview a senior citizen about warm, sad, funny, precious, old, and recent memories.
2. Write these up in a memory book and give to the interviewee after sharing it with the class.

 PUBLISHING

Display memory books on a bulletin board entitled GOLDEN YEARS.

The Wall

Eve Bunting

Clarion Books, 1990

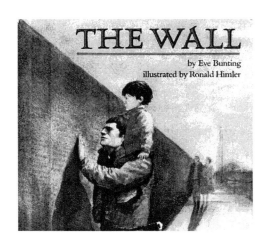

**Memorial Day May 30
(often observed on the last Monday in May)**

Artifact: A pencil rubbing

Summary: A father and son visit the Vietnam Veterans Memorial in Washington, D.C. There they find the name of the boy's grandfather, who was killed in the conflict.

READING/WRITING CONNECTIONS

1. Write the word *memorial* on the board. Create a word web of associations. Then explain that Memorial Day, once called Decoration Day, began when people decorated the graves of those who died in the Civil War. Today Americans remember and honor the dead of all wars.
2. Show the front cover of the book. Discuss. Show the back cover. Discuss.
3. After reading the book, let students do pencil rubbings like the one in the book. They place two pieces of paper on top of one another. Pressing heavily on the top sheet, they print their names. After removing the top sheet, an impression will be seen in the second page. Then they put a sheet of tracing paper, thin typing paper, or Oriental paper over the impression and rub over it with the side of a soft pencil.
4. Under the pencil rubbing, students write to the family or friend of a person who died while serving in the armed forces. Share.

EXTENSIONS

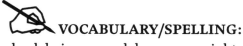 **VOCABULARY/SPELLING:**

wheelchair   medals   weighted   proud   soldiers

 LIBRARY CONNECTIONS

1. Display books involving United States armed conflicts. Discuss. Locate, in an atlas or on a map or globe, the sites of wars in which the United States was involved.
2. If possible, make available *The Wall: Images and Offerings from the Vietnam Veterans Memorial* conceived by Sal Lopes. This book captures feelings and images about the Vietnam Veterans Memorial (often called The Wall) through photography and extends Bunting's book.

 INTEGRATED ACTIVITY

1. Provide students with data about the wall. In groups, students create either a mathematical word problem entailing computations, or a social studies problem requiring research.

   58,132 names listed chronologically according to their deaths appear on two walls.
   Each wall is 246.75 feet long.
   They meet at an angle of 125 degrees.
   The walls are 10.1 feet high.
   Each wall has 70 panels.
   The wall was conceived by Jan C. Scruggs.
   The wall was designed by Maya Ying Lin.
2. Exchange with other groups. Groups work out answers.

PUBLISHING

Create a black bulletin board titled THE WALL. Display rubbings and writing done by students. Add books, pictures, letters, flags and anything else related to Memorial Day.

48
Dr. JAC

I Wish I Were a Butterfly

James Howe

Harcourt Brace Jovanovich, 1987

Summer Solstice
June 21 or 22

Artifact: A miniature butterfly (available in craft stores)

Summary: A cricket with low self-esteem is helped by a wise spider.

READING/WRITING CONNECTIONS

1. Introduce the book by asking students to think about summer. Explain that today is the summer solstice. Today the earth is tilted so that the North Pole is its closest to the sun, so the summer solstice is the longest day of the year and the shortest night. Tell them you have a special book to share to help celebrate this season.

2. Hold the book open so students get the full effect of the butterfly on the dust jacket. Write the word *butterfly* on the board and ask students to brainstorm words that describe it. When someone offers *beautiful,* use that adjective to encourage deeper thinking about the nature of beauty and what makes something beautiful.

3. Review the elements of a narrative. Review the beginning of Howe's story and what he does to draw the reader into the story. Discuss the effectiveness of the ending.

4. Distribute a miniature butterfly to each student and ask each student to write a sequel to Howe's story. They are to begin with, "What beautiful music that creature makes. I wish I were a cricket." They may want to continue with the theme of beauty , or they may want to write about summer, but a butterfly should be in the story. Share.

EXTENSIONS

VOCABULARY/SPELLING:

crickets	fiddler	defiantly	scolded	sighed	butterfly
argue	glowworm	inspecting	handsomest	ugliest	lightning
reflection	mirrored	dragonfly	magnificent	whispery	beautiful

LIBRARY CONNECTIONS

1. Share two books with students that extend Howe's book:
     ❖Eric Carle's *The Very Quiet Cricket*
     ❖Maria M. Mudd's *The Butterfly*.
   Complete a Venn Diagram on these insects' characteristics. Discuss.
2. Take students on a nature hunt. Divide students into teams. They list as many beautiful things as they can find during this walk. Caution students that they should be prepared to defend their choices. After the walk, share lists and discuss the choices.
3. Write wish lists. Share. Talk about wishes, why we make them, how they make us feel.

 INTEGRATED ACTIVITY

1. Students may research some of the butterflies of the tropical rain forest: Scamander, *Anteos menippe*, Passion-flower, *Siproeta stelenes*, *Papilio androgeus*, *Hamadryas arinome,* Blue morpho, *Vindula arsinoe*, and Urania.
2. To share their research, students anthropomorphise their butterflies by attributing human characteristics to them. That way the subject of their research can talk, think, and feel.

 PUBLISHING

Construct a huge butterfly (wire works well). Suspend it from the ceiling in the middle of the room with students' work hanging from it for a SUMMER FLUTTERS BY display.

"Autumnal Equinox"

Edward E. Wilson

Paul Janeczko's *The Music of What Happens: Poems that Tell Stories.*

Orchard Books, 1988

Autumnal Equinox
September: On or about the 23rd

Grade level: 6-12

Artifact: A tri-folded response paper

Summary: The narrator tells about how an experience at harvest time jolted him from his childhood into adulthood.

READING/WRITING CONNECTIONS

1. Inform students today is autumnal equinox, and day and night will be of equal length all over the world. Before reading the poem, remind students to listen carefully so they can participate in a tri-fold response following the reading.
2. Read the poem. Without discussion, students fold a plain sheet of paper in thirds.
3. In the middle third, students write what struck them most in the poem, for example: an unusual word, an image, a phrase, something they remember in the poem.
4. In the top third, students write whatever happened before what they wrote in the middle section. (If students wrote the first line or the title, they infer what came before.)
5. In the lower third, students write whatever happened after what they wrote in the middle section. (If students wrote the last line or word, they predict what happens next.)
6. Divide students in small groups. Each student shares his or her paper by reading the middle section first, then the other two sections. Discuss what is alike and different in the responses. As a class, discuss what caused those like and different responses.

EXTENSIONS

 VOCABULARY/SPELLING:

shocks	funnies	sandwiched	makeshift	turf
trailer	tight-rope style	hardened	bazooka	parallel

 **LIBRARY CONNECTIONS**

1. Divide students into groups. Ask groups to arrive at consensus on two things: the approximate year the story in the poem takes place and the geographical location of the poem. Students may check or research any details in the poem as they discuss possibilities.

2. Help students use library resources to check on other things from the poem that might help group consensus, such as the authenticity of a Swisher County, when "Dear Abby" appeared in the newspapers, in what area of the country would people be interested in hog futures, the years the Packers played, and information on Honda and Yamaha motorcycles.

3. Groups share their decisions, explaining their reasons. Discuss.

 INTEGRATED ACTIVITY

Divide the class in half. One half writes persuasively in favor of the poem's title; the other half writes persuasively that the title does not work.

PUBLISHING

Share persuasive pieces then tack the pros on one side of a corn shock that has been affixed to the center of a bulletin board and the cons on the other. Title the display AUTUMNAL EQUINOX.

The Best of Poetry Books

This Same Sky: A
Collection of Poems from
Around the World

Selected by Naomi Shihab Nye

Four Winds Press, 1992

Grade level: 5-12

Artifact: A bit of sawdust

Summary: Herself a poet, Shihab Nye has collected poems from 129 poets representing 68 different countries, all joined under the same sky. In this truly unique and multi-cultural anthology, readers meet poets from the Chinese poet Gu Cheng, who wants "every instant to be as lovely as crayons," to the Irish poet Maire Mhac an tSaoi, who reminds readers that "tying your shoe is only the first tying."

READING/WRITING CONNECTIONS

1. Show the dust jacket. Encourage speculation about the illustration, the title, and the sub-title. Examine the end papers. Explain that when Naomi Shihab Nye invited poets to send entries for this collection, she asked them for their signatures. Many are included along with the stamps from their countries on the end papers. See how many countries the students can identify by looking at the stamps.

2. Divide students into groups. Put some sawdust on paper in the middle of the group. Encourage students to experience the sawdust. Talk about how it smells, what memories it evokes, its origin. Conclude by asking, "Does sawdust serve any purpose? Would you compare it to poetry?" Discuss.

3. Explain that Jaan Kaplinski from Estonia wrote a poem that compares poetry and sawdust. Read her untitled poem on page 9. Have students write a response to the poem or to Kaplinski sawdust simile; they may write another poem as response, or they may create their own simile for poetry. Share.

 WRITING POETRY: Letter Poems

1. Several of the poems in this collection are dedicated to specific people. Read one or two as models: "Sweet Like a Crow" by Michael Ondaatje for Hetti Corea, 8 years old, "Salt and Memory" by Zoltan Zelk, written as a tribute to Marc Chagall, or "For

Genevieve (Five Years Old) " by Simeon Dumdum, Jr.

2. Discuss these letter-like poems. Help students understand that these poems are like a one-sided conversation; they are written as though the other person were actually present. These poems have an authentic quality to them; they are not abstract; they say real things.

3. Brainstorm people to whom students could write a letter poem : relatives, historical personages, friends, someone deceased. Nudge the students to be specific: Aunt Helen, Booker T. Washington, Grandmom, Babe Ruth, Moses. (This may easily be connected to a literature or social studies lesson by having students choose from those people being studied.)

4. After brainstorming, students write a letter poem to someone they choose.

 PUBLISHING

Students create a class book after the manner of THIS SAME SKY. They design a cover, collaborate on a title, and simulate endpapers with signatures. The book should contain a title page, complete with a publishing company; a copyright page; a dedication; and a table of contents. The cooperative effort of compiling the book supports the idea of all people under the same sky.

51

Neighborhood Odes

Gary Soto
    Illustrator: David Diaz

Harcourt Brace Jovanovich, 1992

Grade level: 7-12

Artifact: A pomegranate seed

Summary: Soto highlights the delights of growing up in an Hispanic neighborhood through these 21 odes. Diaz's black-and-white illustrations accompany the poems in the manner of *papel picado* ("pierced paper") and captures the feel of Mexican-American folk art. The book also contains a glossary of Spanish words and phrases.

READING/WRITING CONNECTIONS

1. Divide students into small groups. Hold up a pomegranate for all to see. Cut it open and place several pomegranate seeds on paper towels in the middle of each group. Students brainstorm by describing the seeds, tasting them; identifying the fruit and the seeds; or associating the pomegranate with some literary or actual experience, such as ancient myths, the Old Testament, or the first time they saw a pomegranate. Share their responses.

2. Explain that the ode has a long literary history. It began as an intricate song bound by formal rules praising gods, heroes, or victorious athletes. By the nineteenth-century, the ode became less formal and more personal, and was often lyrical and long, permitting meditation on some object, event, thing, or person. Contemporary poets have modernized the ode by using free verse and lists of images that usually illuminate a meaning.

3. Introduce Gary Soto's "Ode to Pomegranates." Upon first reading, encourage students to simply experience the poem. Upon second reading, ask students to listen for Soto's rich images and words of praise and jot down the ones that strike them most. Talk about these.

WRITING POETRY
The Ode

1. To ease the writing of the ode, first point out that often odes are like lists with the poet commenting or explaining the meaning of this poetic inventory. All good odes balance the personal and the public, the emotional and the intellectual. Note how Soto saves the last sentence for the public declaration, the message.

2. Students list favorite people, foods, clothes, music, possessions, places, books, classes, hobbies and so forth. They reread their lists, explore their feelings about each, and circle one favorite they would like to praise in an ode.

3. Students then list everything they can think of about that particular favorite. Sometimes using phrases such "to the." "by the," repeated similes ("like a"), or quite simply "I remember" will keep the flow going.

4. When they have exhausted their lists, they pick and choose what they consider best, expanding their lists into the lines of an ode (at least one full page).

5. They incorporate or add their commentary, thereby connecting their topic to the point of the poem.

PUBLISHING

Using one piece of 11" x 17" heavyweight black paper and one piece of the same size light-weight white paper, the students create a *papel picado* page for their ode. They cut the white paper in half. On one half they write their ode; on the other half they create a design by folding the pieces into small sections (the smaller the sections the more intricate the pattern) and cutting out designs along the folded edges. They fold the black paper like a book, and then paste the *papel picado* on one side and the ode on the other. Display under the heading Our Neighborhood Ode.

52

Where the Sidewalk Ends

Shel Silverstein

Harper and Row, 1974

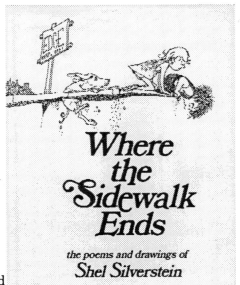

Grade level: Pre-K-5

Artifact: A piece of sidewalk chalk (or colored chalk)

Summary: This classic Silverstein captures objects and events in a child's world through words and drawings. Sometimes the poems are funny, fantastic, or less frightening out where the sidewalk ends, but always they are understandable.

READING/WRITING CONNECTIONS

1. Choose poems to read aloud. (Better to give titles and let the students decide, or, if they know the book, let them suggest their favorites.) If the students know the poems, encourage them to chime in as you read along. Conclude with the title poem. Talk about what kinds of things people do on sidewalks. What do we see on sidewalks? Point out that *sidewalks* is a compound word. Take it apart. Examine what each part of the word means. Why do we have sidewalks? How did they come about? Were sidewalks more important in the past than they are now? Why would Silverstein take readers to "where the sidewalk ends"? Invite students to speculate on what he might mean by that.

2. Divide students into four or five "sidewalk groups." Distribute long sheets of butcher paper (if possible, different colors to different groups). Students participate in a "chalk-in." They create a sidewalk and write or draw their thoughts and feelings on it. Play some background music as students work.

3. Students choose where to display their sidewalks. After they make their choice, be certain to ask them why they chose that place (floor, wall, ceiling, hall). Honor their choices.

WRITING POETRY: Fun and Games

1. Brainstorm games students might play outside on a sidewalk, or driveway: hop scotch, basketball, ball blocks, jump rope, jacks, tag, and so forth. Invite students to tell how each game is played. Talk about playing games, the difference between playing outside and inside, having fun, being outside in the yard or on the sidewalk.

2. Discuss "where the sidewalk ends" (literally or symbolically), where games may be made up such as playing house, making mud pies, or pretending to be a dancer or cowboy or cowgirl. Students enact the games through dramatic play.

3. Divide students into groups of three for role playing: Two play friends while one plays another person who might answer the phone (mother, grandfather, baby-sitter). Students role play calling a friend on the telephone to invite that person to come over to play a sidewalk game. The friend does not answer the phone; instead, the other person answers. Practice telephone manners.

4. Together create a game. First list possible titles, such as dolls, stick tag, hide the rock. Choose one game from the list. Write the rules of the game suggested by the students on sentence strips and place in pocket charts. Test the game. Make revisions. When the game is complete, play it.

5. Students write about a game. They may write about one they know, change it, add variations, or create a new game.

 PUBLISHING

Students come to the author's chair with their writing. They read and receive the applause. Afterward, display the writing in the room under the title WHERE OUR SIDEWALK BEGINS.

53

Dr. JAC

Arithmetic

Carl Sandburg
Illustrated as an anamorphic
adventure by Ted Rand

Harcourt Brace Jovanovich,
Publishers, 1993

Grade level: 3-6

Artifact: A number eraser (available from Oriental
Trading Co., see bibliography)

Summary: Through the anamorphic drawings of Ted Rand, Carl Sandburg's classic
poem assumes a truly contemporary quality. The book comes with a full explanation
of anamorphic drawings, and directions for students to follow when making them.

READING/WRITING CONNECTIONS

1. Divide students into groups according to their number erasers. For example, all twos form a group.

2. Each group generates a list of things they associate with their number or numbers in general. Allot three minutes. As each group shares, the other groups listen for something they have on their list that was not mentioned by a previous group. Successive groups only share the new things on their list.

3. Suggest that associating numbers may have been the way Sandburg got his idea for a poem about arithmetic. Read the poem. (It also may be found as a poem in *Reflections on a Gift of Watermelon Pickle...* by Dunning, et. al. referenced in bibliography.) Discuss.

4. Show the book and read the poem; do not show the pictures. Then read it again showing the illustrations. Ask students how the words and illustrations go together. After responses, read the section that explains anamorphic drawing (precisely stretched or condensed images). Speculate why Rand chose this poem for his drawings.

5. Rotate groups so one group gets to experience the book, while other groups try to create anamorphic drawings with grids and with the Mylar sheet. (If possible, try to locate additional Mylar sheets.)

6. Conclude by testing the notion mentioned in the book that most people are "lazy lookers." Form a circle. Place ten to fifteen familiar objects in the center. Everyone looks carefully at the objects for one minute. Remove the objects. Students return to

their seats and write down what they remember seeing. Share and discuss results.

WRITING POETRY: Anaphora

1. Distribute copies of the poem "Arithmetic." Examine the structure of the poem with students. Ask them to underline the sentences in the poem and highlight the first words in each sentence. Then challenge students to find a pattern. (Most students will immediately see that six of the nine sentences begin with the same word *Arithmetic,* and that the other three sentences begin with the same two words, *If you.*) Tell them this pattern of repetition is called *anaphora,* a Greek word used to describe lines, clauses, or sentences that begin with the same word or almost the same word. Use the poetry of Walt Whitman for an example of anaphora.

2. Students make a list of subjects they study such as music, science, ballet, karate. Each student chooses one of these and creates a poem using anaphora. They use Sandburg's poem as a model.

3. When they have completed the final revisions on their poems, encourage them to create at least one anamorphic drawing as an illustration.

PUBLISHING

Cover a bulletin board, wall, or hallway area with aluminum foil. Display students poems and illustrations. Title the display: ANAMORPHIC POEMS WITH A HINT OF ANAPHORA.

54

Tomie dePaola's Book of Poems

Anthologized by Tomie dePaola

G. P. Putnam's Sons, 1988

Grade level: PreK-5 (bi-or multilingual)

Artifact: A snail shell (available in gourmet food and craft stores)

Summary: This exuberant collection of poetry combines delightful poems with Tomie dePaola's art. Poems range from the classics of Lewis Carroll, William Blake, and others to contemporary poets such as Byrd Baylor and Dorothy Aldis. Also represented are several multicultural selections.

READING/WRITING CONNECTIONS

1. Write the words *caracola, escargot,* and *snail* on the board. Ask how many students can read all three words. Ask whether anyone in the class knows that word in another language. Add to the list.

2. Read Frederico Garcia Lorca's poem, "Caracola" in Spanish or invite a volunteer to read. Read the poem "Snail" in English. Talk about how the poem begins and ends. Encourage students to talk about what they think the poem means. Ask what students think of dePaola's illustration.

3. Distribute the snail shells. Students examine them closely. Tell students the snail is a gastropod mollusk with a spiral shell. There are thousands of species on land and in water. Some species are eaten. Encourage students to run their fingers around and inside the shell.

4. Students divide a notebook-size sheet of paper into five narrow columns. They label each column: "See," "Hear, " "Touch," "Smell, " "Taste. " Under each heading they write the appropriate sense perceptions they get from their shell. For example, for taste, they may write what they think the shell (or its contents) might taste like. Share.

 **WRITING POETRY**

Bilingual Poetry

1. Divide students into groups so that there is a bilingual student in each group. Together they compose a poem, however brief, about some living thing, such as a cactus, bird, horse.

2. If there are no bilingual or multilingual students in the class, bring in dictionaries of other languages and let students translate another poem from the book or compose one in English and then translate it into another language. This is a wonderful way to validate other languages and encourage students to appreciate other languages and cultures.

3. Students write their poems on colored paper that they have cut to resemble the shape of whatever their poem is about, such as a caterpillar, snail, or butterfly. (Use students' versions; avoid precut versions.)

4. Explain that just as poems have layers of language and meaning, so, too, does art. One type of layered art is the *mola*, a brightly colored design that is made of layers of colors placed one on top of another. Each design is cut a bit larger than the one before, which gives it a dimensional look. *Molas* date back to the early 1900's and the Cuna Indians of Panama, who created *molas* out of fabric.

5. Students find five or six different colors that they like. They lay the poem design on top of one color and trace the shape a little bigger. Then they place that design on another color and trace the shape a little bigger still. Repeat through all five or six colors. Paste the designs together one on top of the other with the biggest on the bottom and the poem on top.

 PUBLISHING

Students display their poems on walls or bulletin boards under the heading POEM *MOLAS!*

La Nochebuena South of the Border

James Rice

Pelican Publishing Company, 1993

Grade level: All levels

Artifact: A piece of red material (from Papa Noel's serape)

Summary: This bilingual (English/Spanish) version of "The Night Before Christmas," with Papa Noel as Santa Claus and the reindeer and sleigh replaced with a cart drawn by eight burros, is written in both English and Spanish.

READING/WRITING CONNECTIONS

1. Distribute pieces of red material. Tell students that as you read *La Nochebuena South of the Border* they are to listen carefully in order to figure out the artifact connection. Read the English version of the Christmas poem.

2. Divide students into small groups. Each group generates a list of all the red things in the poem, decides on the most likely item, and stars that item. Share lists and choices. Validate *serape as* the correct response.

3. Write *serape* on board or chart and together define the word. With some non-Spanish speaking students, it may be necessary to figure out the word's meaning through contextual or visual clues.

4. Explain that inserting Spanish words into an English text is called code-switching, something all bilingual speakers do, orally and in writing. Be certain to affirm code-switching as enriching and not something wrong.

5. Add other Spanish words that Rice code-switched to a word bank, preferably one designed with some Christmas motif.

 **WRITING POETRY**

Code-switching

1. Working in groups, students have several choices. They may write:
   - a different adaptation of "The Night Before Christmas" in English, code-switching in any language;
   - a different adaptation of "The Night Before Christmas" in English using the Spanish words in the word bank for the code-switch;
   - the original version of this Christmas poem and code-switch words in Spanish or another language;
   - Rice's version and code-switch words in a language other than Spanish.

2. Visit the library so students may use various sources to research words in other languages.

 PUBLISHING

Students create piñata poems. Each group:
   - inserts their poem into a balloon, which they blow up and tie;
   - covers the balloon with strips of newspaper that have been dipped into art glue;
   - allows the newspaper-covered balloon to dry;
   - decorates the balloon with paint, colored glue, fringed tissue paper, or whatever and pops the balloon
   - suspends the piñata from the classroom ceiling around a banner displayed flat on the ceiling that says "Our Pinata Poems." At some point students share their poems at a Piñata Poetry Party !

How Does the Wind Walk

Nancy White Carlstrom
Illustrator: Deborah Kogan

Macmillan Publishing Company, 1993

Grade level: 3-5 or upper grades to introduce parallelism and antithesis

Artifact: A leaf print

Summary: A little boy notices how the wind "walks" throughout the different seasons. He exults in the wind and joyfully meets each new challenge.

READING/WRITING CONNECTIONS

1. Take students on a brief leaf-choosing walk or bring a box filled with different varieties of leaves. Students choose one or several they like or find interesting.
2. After covering the work area with newspapers, students arrange their leaf or leaves on a piece of construction paper, paint the back of the leaf or leaves with tempera, place white or light-colored construction paper on top of the wet paint, press down on it, and lift the paper to reveal the print. (Remove any leaves that stick.)
3. With that preparation, introduce the book. Ask students to connect the book's cover with the activity. Discuss.
4. Read the autumn section. Students write their responses to that section around their leaf print. Share. Display.

WRITING POETRY
Parallelism and Antithesis

1. Invite students to predict the contents of the remainder of the book. Read to test their predictions.
2. Ask students to identify the pattern in the book: a question followed by stanzas about the wind and a boy.
3. Once the pattern is identified, ask students to look more closely for sub-patterns such as: a question introduces each season. It is written the same way except for the sea-

son's name. The stanzas are written similarly, often with the same parts of speech, words, phrases, clauses. The boy stanza presents an exception.

4. Draw two long parallel lines vertically on board or chart. Write "How does the wind walk in autumn?" next to one line; write, "How does the wind walk in winter?" next to the other line. Continue with other parallels students find in the poem. Help students understand that using these corresponding syntactical forms and constructions in poetry is called parallelism.

5. Draw a line horizontally through the parallel lines about two-thirds of the way down. Write the word *but* on that line. Call students attention to the word *but* that introduces the boy stanza in autumn, winter, and spring. Ask what *but* does. When they see that it sets up a contrast, introduce antithesis. Underline the prefix *anti-*. Explain that this contrast adds interest or tension to the poem. Ask students how the poet sets up the contrast in the summer section. Use their responses to point out that effective parallelism and antithesis do not require a rigid point-for-point correspondence.

6. Suggest that students try writing a poem with parallelism and antithesis. Brainstorm possible topics, for example, sports, TV shows, places at the mall, and animals.

 PUBLISHING

Using a technique sometimes called "poor man's laminating" (which students usually like because they do it themselves), students write their poems, place them between two pieces of waxed paper, press with a warm iron to seal in the poem, trim and glue onto a larger piece of construction paper to make a frame. Share and post as GALLERY OF PARALLEL POEMS

The Napping House

Audrey Wood
Illustrator: Don Wood

Harcourt Brace Jovanovich,
1984

Grade level: PreK-5

Artifact: A clicker

Summary: In this cumulative rhyme that already has become a classic, Audrey Wood tells a simple tale about a cozy bed, a snoring granny, a dreaming child, a dozing dog, a snoozing cat, a slumbering mouse, and a wakeful flea. The flea creates a commotion that delights students of all ages.

READING/WRITING CONNECTIONS

1. Gather students around. Begin by singing the Johannes Brahms lullaby that begins,"Lullaby and goodnight…" Invite students to sing or hum along.
2. Write the word *lullaby* on the board. Draw the definition from students by focusing on the sound of the word *lull*. Talk about how that *L* sound makes them feel.
3. With younger students, brainstorm associations with the word. List in a column on a board or chart. Older students may work in brainstorming groups.
4. With younger students, brainstorm another list of words that describe what might disturb a lullaby or might disturb someone sleeping. Older students may work in brainstorming groups.
5. Transition to the book "where everyone is sleeping." Tell students to listen for what disturbs this "napping house." Begin humming the lullaby again; then read the book. Talk about the colors and shapes of the illustrations.
6. Distribute clickers. Divide students into groups: flea, mouse, cat, dog, child, granny. As they listen to the second reading of the book, the assigned group clicks their clickers three times after their character. When the bed breaks, all the students click their clickers to create a real commotion.

WRITING POETRY: Musicality in Poetry

1. Together with younger students, add other characters to the book. For example, they may suggest adding a parakeet or a bear. Decide on a word to describe what they suggest, such as a *resting* parakeet or *hibernating* bear. Discuss ways to fit their ideas to the poem. For example, the parakeet may land on the granny's nose or the bear may knock over the bedstand. Work that into the cumulative rhyme.

2. Older students may work in groups of two and three to create a totally different variation of the napping house. For example, they may suggest, "There is a mall, a busy mall, where everyone is shopping, " and go from there.

3. Both younger and older students work in groups to make musical instruments to accompany their renditions. Use Margaret McLean's *Make Your Own Musical Instruments* (see bibliography) for easy step-by-step directions. Each group chooses from among castanets, drums, xylophones, various wind instruments, zithers, and others.

 PUBLISHING

Students perform their renditions of *The Napping House* to the accompaniment of their musical instruments. Write invitations to parents and administrators or invite another class to the performance. Call the performance MUSIC, MIRTH, AND MERRYMAKING.

58

The Ballad of Belle Dorcas

William H. Hooks
Illustrator: Brian Pinkney

Alfred A. Knopf, 1990

Grade level: 6-12

Artifact: A piece of scratch board

Summary: This book is based on a tale that evolved from the Gullah people, who live along the Carolina coast. Although not in poetic form, this book provides the foundation for work in ballads because it encapsulates the characteristics of a ballad.

READING/WRITING CONNECTIONS

1. Read the author's note as an introduction. Explain that *Belle Dorcas* is a folk ballad, which is a story usually told as entertainment and as a way to keep alive the beliefs and traditions of the masses. Generally "ballad" means any poem composed to be sung or recited, but the folk ballad usually refers specifically to poems with origins in England, Scotland, Australia, and America.

2. After the reading, distribute scratch boards. Students scratch their version of the story's end and use oil pastels for the colors, which they apply and then wipe off. (If scratch board and oil pastels are not available, a simulation may be achieved by coloring a page with different colors of crayons, totally covering it with back crayon and then scratching out the picture.)

3. After students create their picture, they write a brief explanation. Share and display.

 WRITING POETRY

The Ballad

1. Divide the class into four groups to do library research on the ballad form.

   • One group finds the Scottish ballad "Bonny Barbara Allen." They prepare to sing at least one stanza for the class.

   • The second group researches the ballad stanza, closely related to the common meter, found in such hymns as "Amazing Grace" by the eighteenth-century English hymnist John Newton. The group presents the rhythmic pattern and sings at least a section of a representative ballad in that rhyme scheme.

- The third group looks up "broadside ballads" and "doggerel." They explain the origins of these forms and present an example of each. (Some country/western ballads fall into this category as do songs such as "Pretty Polly.")
- The fourth group finds examples of literary ballads. They define them and present a reading for the class. (This ballad is *not* sung.) Examples may be Housman's "The True Lover" or Keats' "Belle Dame Sans Merci."

2. After research on ballads, together generate a list of the ballad's characteristics: social and political issues, usually tragic in outcome (love, death, domestic tragedy); narrative; sketchy characters; dialogue; often includes incremental repetition, abrupt transitions, and oversimplified plots. Ballads are easy to understand and their message is clear.

3. Students working in groups may choose from these options: Take the book *The Ballad of Belle Dorcas* and write it as a poetic ballad, write an original ballad, or write an analysis of a classic ballad such as "Sir Patrick Spence."

 PUBLISHING

Because broadside ballads were printed on one sheet of paper, students write their final drafts on one sheet using any layout they feel is appropriate, keeping in mind that these ballads are considered an early form of journalism. Students participate in a SHARE AROUND in which the ballads may be read, sung, or recited to live or taped music.

Sheep in a Jeep

Nancy Shaw
Illustrator: Margot Apple

Houghton Mifflin
Company, 1986

Grade level: PreK-1

Artifact: A piece of wool yarn

Summary: This classic book records the misadventures of five sheep as they go riding in a jeep. The story is told in rollicking rhyme accompanied by delightful illustrations that bring the sheep and the other animals to life.

READING/WRITING CONNECTIONS

1. Show students the double-spread cover. Encourage students to talk about the illustration. Spend time raising their awareness of what is the same and what is different in the illustrations. Ask them to describe each of the sheep, identify the other two animals pictured, and predict what they think the book may be about. Talk about the jeep; its color; how it is like a car, bus, or other vehicles; and how it is unlike a car, bus, or other vehicles.

2. Continue nudging this oral awareness throughout the title pages. Ask what each sheep is doing, and why two might be looking in the same direction.

3. Read the book, pausing to permit students to interact.

4. When the reading is complete, make certain the students understand why the jeep ended up in a heap.

5. Distribute the wool yarn. Together recite the nursery rhyme "Baa, Baa Black Sheep." Talk about sheep as the origin of wool.

6. Students write or draw their own sheep in a jeep or, depending upon where they are developmentally, they may draw their sheep in some other vehicle or engaged in some other pastime other than that pictured in the book. They paste their wool yarn on their sheep. Share, and then display.

WRITING POETRY:
Long "E" Sound (e̅e̅)

1. Our speech sounds are divided into vowels and consonants. Vowels are like musical notes that may be set up like a musical scale according to frequency. The e̅e̅ sound is at the top of the scale because it has a high frequency; it is busier, gives the ear more to process than its cousins the o̅o̅ or o̅ which are at the bottom of the scale.

2. Take students through the vowel scale. Make it fun to say the words:

   boo! (o̅o̅), bone (o̅), book (ŏŏ), bought (aw) , boy (oi), bough (ow), bar (ar) ,

   bud (ŭ), bird (ur), bat (ă), bet (ĕ), bit (ĭ), buy (ī), bay (ā), bee (e̅e̅).   —

3. Reenter the book. Invite students to read the words with all the energy of the ee sound.

4. Set up a chair in the room as the jeep. Students role play the story, periodically saying, "Beep! Beep!" and other words and lines from the story.

5. After role playing, brainstorm words that have the e̅e̅ sound, both from the story and those not used in the story: *steep, deep, keep, sleep,* and so on.

6. Write a class poem together that extends the book and uses the words from the brainstormed list. For example, they may suggest, "Sheep keep the jeep. Sheep sleep. Sheep sleep deep. Sheep dream about a jeep." Provide plenty of opportunity for language play with the e̅e̅ sound.

 PUBLISHING

The sheep made a "For Sale" sign for their jeep. Students make "For Sale" signs for their poems. They choose their paper, their colors, and where they want to hang their signs. Label this display OUR POEMS ARE NOT CHEAP!

The Music of What Happens: Poems that Tell Stories

Selected by Paul B. Janeczko

Orchard Books, 1988

Grade level: 9-12

Artifact: A Star of David

Summary: This collection offers narrative poems by contemporary authors such as Gary Soto, Stephen Dunn, Robert Pack, Erika Mumford, and Rita Dove. An introductory Irish fairy story explains the title, and the opening poem states the purpose of poetry.

READING/WRITING CONNECTIONS

1. Begin with a series of trigger words. Say the word and give students 30 seconds to 1 minute to write a response. Students may write definitions, associations, clauses, phrases, or sentences. They write quickly following their thoughts. At this point, they do not worry about **spelling** or punctuation, because the purpose is to tap ideas. The trigger words are *white rose*; *snow white, pine cones, Sophie, Führer, Germany, Nazi, Kristallnacht, resistance,* and *chocolate.* After each word, call on one or two students to share what they have written.

2. Distribute cover-stock paper and yellow markers, crayons, glue, or neon paint. Students make a star of David (a six-pointed star) on the paper. Explain that this will serve as the cover for a log they will keep while listening and responding to the 33-part poem "The White Rose: Sophie Scholl 1921-1943" by Erika Mumford.

3. As an introduction to the poem, spend some time discussing the background of Nazi Germany and the students' revolt at the University of Munich. Talk about the anti-Nazi propaganda generated by these students and the Gestapo's reaction to their resistance to the Nazi Party.

3. Read the poem in six sections (I-V, VI-VII, VIII, IX-XI, XII-XX, XXI-XXXIII) over six-days, one section and one day for each point on the Star of David. After each section, students write their responses in their logs, much the way they responded to the trigger words. Invite several students to share their entries. Discuss.

WRITING POETRY: Historical Poems

1. Students engage in research about World World II , the holocaust, and Hans and Sophie Scholl . (See references to Shirer's *The Rise and Fall of the Third Reich* and Von Hassell's *The Von Hassell Diaries* in the bibliography.)

2. In groups, students analyze their research in light of the poem. Discuss the implications of accurate information when writing a historical poem.

3. Brainstorm interesting historical people or events as possible topics for a historical poem. People and events may be linked to whatever era is being studied in social studies or in literature, such as the Great Depression, the Puritans, or the Renaissance.

4. Students, working individually or in groups, research a character or event in more detail and work on a historical poem. Use "The White Rose: Sophie Scholl 1921-1943" as a model.

 PUBLISHING

In keeping with the information in the poem, students write their poems as flyers. If they are writing about a different historical period, they may create a publication that fits the era, such as on parchment, in scrolls, in calligraphy, as a newspaper, or between the pages of an old leather book. Call the display: WE'RE MAKING HISTORY!

Emily

Michael Bedard
Illustrator:
Barbara Cooney

A Doubleday Book
for Young Readers,
1992

Grade level: 7-12

Artifact: A copy of Emily's note (in an envelope)

Summary: When neighbor and her daughter visit Emily Dickinson, there is a poetic exchange of gifts. In this poignantly powerful book, readers receive a glimpse of the reclusive poet as seen through the eyes of a child.

READING/WRITING CONNECTION

1. Begin with five trigger words. Students respond freely to *myth, snow, lily bulbs, Emily,* and *1800*. Share.

2. Explain that although this looks like a children's book, it is much more. Show cover and invite any predictions.

3. After reading the book, including its afterward, ask students to reexamine their responses to the trigger words. How would their responses remain the same? How would they change?

4. Introduce the poetry of Emily Dickinson by discussing Emily's response, "No, you are poetry. This only tries to be." Ask students what they think she means. Also discuss, "I brought you some spring." Talk about children and poetry. Get to the question: What is poetry?

5. Distribute copies of the note (poem) Emily wrote. Invite students to write their thoughts, feelings, interpretations, or a response to that note. Share.

WRITING POETRY
Simile and Metaphor

1. Explain the difference between simile and metaphor. Simile comes from the Latin meaning *like*; metaphor is the Latin word for *transfer*. Both make comparisons. Similes use *like* or *as* when comparing two things, whereas metaphors imply that one

thing *is* something else, by making a comparison. Give examples from Dickinson's "the Nerves sit ceremonious, like Tombs—" for simile, and from her "Sacrament, The Wardrobe—of our Lord" for metaphor. Students choose several poems by Dickinson to read aloud. These may be chosen from a textbook or from any collection of Dickinson's work.

2. Help students understand metaphor more easily by playing the three-step "Making a Metaphor Game." First, they partner up with someone and agree on two things: something liked and something disliked (ice cream and mowing the lawn). Second, they agree on some way to make what is liked less appealing or what is disliked more appealing so that there is a characteristic to be compared (melted ice cream/ mowing in the shade). Third, they write that into a sentence or a line as a comparison. (Mowing the lawn is melted ice cream on a hot summer day. Mowing the lawn in the shade is ice cream on a hot summer day.) They may "test" their metaphor as a simile by adding *like* or *as*.

3. After practice, students try their hand at making metaphors in poems. At first encourage them to model Dickinson. Her almost consistent use of the quatrain, the four-line stanza, is sometimes helpful. After they become skilled, they may want to try couplets (two-line stanza) or even nonstanzaic verse paragraphs.

 PUBLISHING

Emily Dickinson kept her poems in a bureau drawer, tied with ribbon in little packets that resembled books. After she died, her sister Lavinia found them and prepared them for publication. Bring in an old drawer, or prepare a box to look like a drawer. Students, working in groups, prepare their poems as Dickinson did. Title the drawer OUR CACHE OF POETRY.

ADVENTURES IN COLOR

Hailstones and halibut bones

By MARY O'NEILL
Illustrated by LEONARD WEISGARD

62
Dr. JAC

Hailstones and Halibut Bones

Mary O'Neill

Doubleday & Company, 1961.
(Available as a new edition.)

Grade level: K-5

Artifact: A crayon

Summary: This classic poetry book about purple, gold, black, brown, blue, gray, white, orange, red, pink, green, and yellow culminates with a poem about "The Colors."

READING/WRITING CONNECTION

1. Divide students into small groups. Give each group a large piece of orange paper on which the following questions are randomly written: "What is orange?" "What does orange remind you of?" "What is orange like?" "What does orange taste or feel like?" "Can you hear orange?" Groups brainstorm responses on the paper. Share.
2. Introduce the book. Read "What Is Orange?" Students compare O'Neill's images to what they have written.
3. Distribute crayons. Each student receives his or her color and lists things associated with that color, such as silver is a star. Silver tastes like sparkling water. Use book and group experience as a model. Share.

 WRITING POETRY
Rhythm and Rhyme

1. Introduce rhythm (what X.J. Kennedy calls "beats that repeat") by asking students to listen for the beats that repeat as you bounce a ball in different rhythms: slow, fast, pausing in between bounces, two slow bounces then several fast ones, and so forth.
2. Invite students to tap out other rhythms on their desks. Make the connection between those demonstrations and using words for rhythm.
3. Show "What is Orange?" on an overhead transparency. As you reread the poem, ask students to listen carefully and then point out examples of rhythm and rhyme. (Rhyme, with its repetition of sound, creates one kind of rhythm.)

4. Mark students' responses on the transparency with an orange marker. There is rhythm in the first line of the first sentence and the first line of the second sentence. Both have five words written in the same rhythm. Other beats that repeat are:
   - lines that begin "Orange is";
   - the prepositional phrases that begin "Of the…"; and
   - the two participles at the end of the poem.

   Students will have no difficulty finding the rhyming words.

5. Point out that the poem has seven sentences. Ask the students to find them. Discuss why they think the first sentence is longer and in a different rhyming pattern than the other six. Talk about how boring a poem would be if the rhythm never varied. Use natural rhythms to point out the beats that repeat and how they change: ocean waves and tides; when a horse walks, runs, gallops, canters; or a shift in the wind.

6. Read several other poems. Choose those with slightly different rhythms and rhyme schemes, such as "What Is Gold?" or "What Is Yellow?" so students have other models. Discuss the rhythm and rhyme of each.

7. Each student explores the rhythm of his or her color by writing it several times close together; stopping in mid-word to see what happens, such as *yellowyellowyellowyell…ow;* creating a new name for it; writing it different ways, such as *berrylly blue* or *white-as-the-caps-of-waves-white.*

8. Students work with O'Neill as a model, using their explorations and their research to create their own color poems.

 **PUBLISHING**

Students write their poems on spatter-painted paper. Display under the title OUR COLORFUL POEMS.

Works Cited

Abrams, M. H., et. al. *The Norton Anthology of British Literature, Fifth Edition.* Beowulf, Vol. 1. "Musee des Beaux Arts," Vol. 2. New York: W.W. Norton and Co., 1988.

Ackerman, Karen. *Araminta's Paint Box.* New York: Atheneum, 1990, *The Tin Heart.* New York: Atheneum, 1990.

Ada, Alma Flor. *The Gold Coin.* New York: Atheneum, 1991.

Adrosko, Rita J. *Natural Dyes and Home Dyeing.* Mineola, New York: Dover Publishing, 1971.

Agee, Jon. *The Incredible Painting of Felix Clousseau.* New York: Farrar, Straus & Giroux, 1988.

Ahlberg, Allan, and Janet Ahlberg. *The Clothes Horse and Other Stories.* New York: Penguin Books, 1988; *Each Peach Pear Plum.* New York: Puffin Books, 1978; *The Jolly Postman or Other People's Letters.* Boston: Little, Brown, 1986.

Alcorn, Johnny. *Rembrandt's Beret.* New York: Tambourine Books, 1991.

Alexander, Bryan and Cherry. *An Eskimo Family.* Minneapolis Minn.: Lerner Publications Co., 1985; *The Eskimos.* New York: Crescent Books, 1988.

Aliki. *A Medieval Feast.* New York: Harper & Row, Publishers, 1983.

Anderson, Emily, trans. *Letters of Beethoven.* London: Macmillan, 1961.

Anderson, Lydia. *Immigration.* New York: Franklin Watts, 1981.

Andrews, Jan. *Very Last First Time.* New York: Atheneum, 1986.

Anno, Mitsumasa. *Anno's Medieval World.* New York: Philomel Books, 1979; *Anno's Peekaboo.* New York: Philomel Books, 1987.

Anthony, Rose Marie. *Fun with Choral Speaking.* Englewood, CO:Libraries Unlimited, 1990.

Asch, Frank. *Skyfire.* New York: Simon & Schuster Books for Young Readers, 1984.

Babbitt, Natalie. *Goody Hall.* New York: Farrar, Straus and Giroux, 1986; *Herbert Rowbarge.* New York: Farrar, Straus and Giroux, 1984; *Kneeknock Rise.* New York: Farrar, Straus and Giroux, 1984; *Phoebe's Revolt.* New York: Farrar, Straus and Giroux, 1988; *Tuck Everlasting.* New York: Farrar, Straus and Giroux, 1975.

Bains, Rae. *Simple Machines.* Mahwah, NJ: Troll Associates, 1985.

Baker, Carlos, ed. *Ernest Hemingway: Selected Letters (1917-1961).* New York: Macmillan, 1989.

Baker, Keith. *The Magic Fan.* New York: Harcourt Brace Jovanovich, Publishers, 1989.

Base, Graeme. *Animalia.* New York: Henry N. Abrams, 1987.

Baskin, Hosie and Leonard. *A Book of Dragons.* New York: Alfred A. Knopf, 1985.

Bayer, Jane. *A My Name is ALICE.* New York: Dial Books for Young Readers, 1984.

Baylor, Byrd. *Amigo.* New York: Aladdin Books, 1989; *The Best Town in the World.* New York: Aladdin Books, 1982; *The Desert Is Theirs.* New York: Aladdin Books, 1986; *Everybody Needs a Rock.* New York: Aladdin Books, 1974; *Feet!* Illustrated by Peter Parnall. New York: Macmillan, 1988; *Guess Who My Favorite Person Is.* New York: Aladdin Books, 1977; *Hawk, I'm Your Brother.* New York: Aladdin Books, 1986; *If You Are a Hunter of Fossils.* New York: Aladdin Books, 1980; *I'm in Charge of Celebrations.* New York: Charles Scribner's Sons, 1986; *Moon Song.* New York: Charles Scribner's Sons, 1982; *One Small Bead.* New York: Charles Scribner's Sons, 1992; *The Way to Start a Day.* New York: Aladdin books, 1986; *When the Clay Sings.* New York: Aladdin Books, 1972; *Your Own Best Secret Place.* New York: Charles Scribner's and Sons. 1988.

Beach, Richard. *Writing about Ourselves and Others.* Urbana, Illinois: NCTE and ERIC. 1977.

Bjork, Christina. *Linnea in Monet's Garden.* New York: R & S Books, 1987.

Blizzard, Gladys S. *Come Look With Me.* Charlottesvile, Virginia: Thomasson-Grant. 1990.

Blood, Charles L. & Martin Link. *Goat in the Rug.* New York: Macmillan Publishing Company, 1976.

Bond, Michael. *A Bear Called Paddington.* New York: Dell, 1968.

Boynton, Sandra. *A is for ANGRY.* New York: Workman Publishing, 1983.

Bradman Tony and Margaret Chamberlain. *Look Out, He's Behind You!* New York: G.P. Putnam's Sons, 1988.

Brandt, Keith. *Indian Crafts.* Mahwah, NJ: Troll Associates, 1985; *Indian Homes.* Mahwah, NJ: Troll Associates, 1985.

Brighton, Catherine. *Five Secrets in a Box.* New York: E.P. Dutton, 1987.

Brown, Laurene Krasny, and Marc Brown. *Visiting the Art Museum.* New York: E.P. Dutton, 1986.

Brown, Marc. *Arthur's April Fool.* Boston: Little, Brown and Company, 1983.

Brown, Margaret Wise. *The City Noisy Book.* New York: Harper & Row, 1989; *David's Little Indian.* Birmingham, Alaama: Hopscotch Books, 1989; *The Dead Bird..* New York: Harper & Row, 1958; *Goodnight Moon.* New York: Harper & Row, 1947; *The Important Book.* New York: Harper & Row, 1949; *The Little Fireman.* New York: Harper & Row, 1952; *The Runaway Bunny.* New York: Harper & Row, 1970.

Bruxner, Mervyn. *Letters to a Musical Boy.* London: Oxford University Press, 1966.

Bunting, Eve. *The Wall.* New York: Clarion Books, 1990; *The Wednesday Surprise.* New York: Clarion Books, 1989.

Burns, Marilyn. *Math for Smarty Pants.* Boston: Little, Brown and Company, 1982.

Butterfield, L.H., Marc Friedlande, and Mary-Jo Kline, Eds. *The Books of Abigail and John: Selected Letters of the Adams Family, 1762-1784.* Cambridge, MA: Harvard University Press, 1975.

Butzow, Carol M. and John W. Butzow. *Science through Children's Literature: An Integrated Approach.* Englewood, Colorado: Libraries Unlimited, Inc. 1989.

Caduto, Michael J. and Joseph Bruchac. *Keepers of the Earth: Native American* Stories and Environmental

Activities for Children. Golden, Colorado: Fulcrum, Inc., 1989 (and Teacher's Guide).

Caldecott, Randolph. *A First Caldecott Collection* and *A Second Caldecott Collection.* New York: Warne, 1986.

Campbell, Rod. *My Presents.* New York: Aladdin Books, 1989.

Carle, Eric *Papa, Please Get the Moon for Me.* Natik, MA: Picture Book Studio, 1986; *The Secret Birthday Message.* New York: Harper & Row, 1986; *The Tiny Seed.* Saxonville, MA:Picture Book Studio, 1987; *The Very Quiet Cricket.* New York: Philomel Books, 1990.

Carle, Eric. *Dragons Dragons & Other Creatures That Never Were.* (Compiled by Laura Whipple) New York: Philomel Books, 1991.

Carlstrom, Nancy White. *How Does the Wind Walk?* New York: Macmillan Publishing Company, 1993.

Carrick, Donald. *Morgan and the Artist.* New York: Clarion Books, 1985.

Cazet, Denys. *Frosted Glass.* New York: Bradbury Press, 1987.

Chrisman, Arthur Bowie. *Shen of the Sea: Chinese Stories for Children.* New York: E.P. Dutton, 1925.

Christopher, Matt. *Baseball Pals.* Boston: Little, Brown and Co., 1967; *Catcher with a Glass Arm.* Boston: Little, Brown and Co.,1967; *Look Who's Playing First Base.* Boston: Little, Brown and Co., 1967; *Miracle at the Plate.* Boston: Little, Brown and Co., 1967; *No Arm in Left Field.* Boston: Little, Brown and Co., 1967; *Shortstop from Tokyo.* Boston: Little, Brown and Co., 1967; *The Diamond Champs.* Boston: Little, Brown and Co., 1967; *The Fox Steals Home.* Boston: Little, Brown and Co., 1967; *The Kid Who Only Hits Homers.* Boston: Little, Brown and Co., 1967; *Year Mom Won the Pennant.* Boston: Little, Brown and Co., 1967.

Climo, Shirley. *The Egyptian Cinderella.* Illustrated by Ruth Heller. New York:Thomas Y. Crowell, 1989.

Coerr, Eleanor. *The Josefina Story Quilt.* New York: Harper Collins Publishers, 1986.

Cohlene, Terri. *Turquoise Boy: A Navajo Legend.* Mahwah, NJ: Watermill Press, 1990.

Colgin, Mary Lou, comp. *One Potato, Two Potato, Three Potato, Four: 165 Chants for Children.* Mt. Rainer, MD: Gryphon House, 1982.

Conaway, Judith, and Renzo Barto. *More Science Sevrets.* Mahwah, N.J.: Troll Associates, 1987.

Copland, Aaron. *Lincoln Portrait & Other Works.* (Cincinnati Pops Orchestra, conducted by Erich Kunzel) Cincinnati, Ohio: Telarc (CD-80117), 1987.

Copus, Pamela. *The Ancient Ones.* Dreamtime Productions, P.O. Box 940061, Plano, TX 75094-0061.

Cormier, Robert. *After the First Death.* New York: Pantheon, 1979; *Beyond the Chocolate War.* New York: Knopf, 1985; *Fade.* New York: Delacorte Press, 1988; *I Am the Cheese.* New York: Random House, 1977; *Other Bells for Us to Ring.* New York: Delacorte Press, 1990; *The Bumblebee Flies Anyway.* New York: Dell, 1983; *The Chocolate War.* New York: Dell, 1986; *We All Fall Down.* New York: Delacorte Press, 1991; *Tenderness.* New York: Delacorte Press, 1997.

Cowper, William. *Works of William Cowper.* "Mother Goose Rhymes". Edited by Robert Southey. 15 vol. Reprint of the 1837 edition. New York: AMS Press.

Davidson, Josephine. *Teaching an Dramatizing Greek Myths.* Englewood, Colo.: Libraries Unlimited, 1989.

de Beer, Hans. *Ahoy There, Little Polar Bear.* New York: North-South Books, 1988; *Little Polar Bear.* New York: North-South Books, 1987; *The Little Polar Bear Address Book.* New York: North-South Books, 1990; *The Little Polar Bear Birthday Book.* New York: North-South Books, 1990; *Little Polar Bear Finds a Friend.* New York: North- South Books, 1989.

dePaola, Tomie. *Bonjour, Mr. Satie.* New York: G.P. Putnam's Sons, 1991; *The Art Lesson.* New York: G.P. Putnam's Sons, 1989; *The Legend of the Indian Paintbrush.* New York: G. P. Putnam's Sons, 1988.; *The Popcorn Book.* New York: Holiday House, 1978; *Tomie dePaola's Book of Poems.* New York: G. P. Putnam's Sons, 1988.

de Regnier, Beatrice Schenk, et. al. (eds.) *Sing a Song of Popcorn.* New York: Scholastic, 1988.

De Vries, Leonard. *A Treasury of Illustrated Children's Books: Early Nineteenth-Century Classics from the Osborne Collection.* New York: Abbeville Press, 1989.

Deedy, Carmen Agra. *Agatha's Feather Bed: Not Just Another Wild Goose Story.* Atlanta, Georgia: Peachtree Publishers, Ltd., 1991.

deLarminat, Max-Henri. *Vassily Kandinsky: Sky Blue.* New York: Harry N. Abrams, Inc., 1990.

Demi. *Chingis Khan.* New York: Henry Holt and Company, 1991; *Demi's Opposites: An Animal Game Book.* New York: Grosset & Dunlap, 1987; *Demi's Reflections.* New York: Grosset & Dunlap, 1988; *The Empty Pot.* New York: Grosset & Dunlap, 1990.

Dickinson, Mike. *Smudge.* New York: Abbeville Press, 1987.

Dunning, Stephen, Edward Lueders, Hugh Smith. *Reflections on a Gift of Watermelon Pickle ... and Other Modern Verse.* New York: Lothrop, Lee & Shepard Co., 1967.

Ehlert, Lois. *Color Farm.* New York: J.P. Lippincott, 1990; *Color Zoo.* New York: J. P. Lippincott, 1989; *Eating the Alphabet.* San Diego: Harcourt Brace Jovanovich, 1989; *Feathers for Lunch.* New York: Harcourt Brace Jovanovich, 1990; *Fish Eyes: A Book You Can Count On.* San Diego: Harcourt Brace Jovanovich, 1990; *Grown Vegetable Soup.* New York: Harcourt Brace Jovanovich, 1987; *Planting a Rainbow.* New York: Harcourt Brace Jovanovich, 1988.

Ekoomiak, Normee. *Arctic Memories.* New York: Holt, 1990.

Elting, Mary, and Michael Folsom. *Q is for Duck.* New York: Clarion Books, 1980.

Fair, Sylvia. *The Bedspread.* New York: William Morrow and Company, 1982.

Faulkner, William. *Absalom, Absalom.* New York: McGraw Hill, 1966; *As I Lay Dying.* New York: Random House, 1964; *The Sound and the Fury.* New York: McGraw Hill, 1966.

Flack, Jerry D. *Inventing, Inventions, and Inventors: A Teaching Resource Book.* Englewood, Colo.: Libraries Unlimited, Inc., 1989.

Flack, Marjorie. *Ask Mr. Bear*. New York: Aladdin books, 1986.

Fleischman, Pau.l. *I Am Phoenix: Poems for Two Voices*. New York: Harper & Row, 1985; *Joyful Noise: Poems for Two Voices*. New York: Harper & Row, 1988.

Flournoy, Valerie. *The Patchwork Quilt*. New York: Dial Books, 1985.

Fox, Dan and Claude Marks. *Go In and Out the Window*. New York: Henry Holt and Company, 1987.

Fox, Mem. *Hattie and the Fox*. New York: Bradbury Press, 1988; *Shoes From Grandpa*. New York: Orchard Books, 1989; *Wilfrid Gordon McDonald Partridge*. New York: Kane/Miller Book Publishers, 1985.

Fradon, Dana. *Harold the Herald: A Book About Heraldry*. New York: Dutton's Children's Books, 1990.

Fraser, Antonia, ed. *Love Letters: An Illustrated Anthology*. Chicago, IL: Contemporary Books, 1989.

Freedman, Russell. *Buffalo Hunt*. New York: Holiday Books. 1988; *Children of the Wild West*. New York: Clarion Books. 1983; *Cowboys of the Wild West*. New York: Clarion Books. 1985; *Dinosaurs and Their Young*. New York: Holiday Books. 1983; *Farm Babies*. New York: Holiday Books. 1981; *Franklin Delano Roosevelt*. New York: Clarion Books. 1990; *Immigrant Kids*. New York: E. P. Dutton. 1980; *Indian Chiefs*. New York: Holiday Books. 1987; *Lincoln: A Photobiography*. New York: Clarion Books. 1987; *Rattlesnakes*. New York: Holiday Books. 1984.

Freuchen, Peter. *Book of Eskimos*. New York: Fawcett, 1981.

Fritz, Jean. *Homesick: My Own Story*. New York: G.P. Putnam's Sons, 1984; *Where do you think you're going, Christopher Columbus?* New York: G.P. Putnam's Sons, 1980.

Gackenbach, Dick. *A Bag Full of Pups*. New York: Clarion Books, 1981; *Binky Gets a Car*. New York: Clarion Books, 1983; *Claude and Pepper* New York: Clarion Books, 1976; *Dog for a Day*. New York: Clarion Books, 1987; *Harry and the Terrible Whatzit*. New York: Clarion Books, 1977; *Harvey the Follish Pig*. New York: Clarion Books, 1988; *Hurray for Hattie Rabbit*. New York: Harper & Row, 1986; *Poppy the Panda*. New York: Clarion Books, 1984; *With Love From Gran*. New York: Clarion Books, 1989.

Gardner, Marjory, Heather Philpott and Jane Tanner (illustrators). *Time For a Rhyme*. Australia: Thomas Nelson, 1989.

George, Jean Craighead. *Julie of the Wolves*. New York: Harper & Row, 1972; *Water Sky*. New York: Harper & Row, 1987.

Gerard, John. *The Herbal or General History of Plants*. Mineola, New York: Dover Publishing, 1975.

Gibbons, Gail *How a House Is Built*. New York: Holiday House, 1990; *The Pottery Place*. New York: Harcourt Brace Jovanovich, 1987.

Giff, Patricia Reilly. *Happy Birthday, Ronald Morgan!* New York: Puffin Books, 1988.

Gill, Peter. *Birds*. Mahwah, NJ: Troll Associates, 1990.

Gill, Shelley. *The Alaska Mother Goose*. Homer, Alaska: Paws IV Publishing Company, 1987.

Golenbock, Peter. *Teammates*. New York: Gulliver Books (HBJ), 1990.

Goodall, John S. *The Story of a Main Street*. New York: Margaret K. McElderry Books, 1987.

Graves, Donald H. *Investigate Nonfiction*. Portsmouth, New Hampshire: Heinemann. 1989.

Greaves, Margaret. *The Lucky Coin*. New York: Stewart, Tabori & Chang, Inc., 1989.

Greenaway, Kate. *A: Apple Pie: An Old Fashioned Alphabet Book*. London: Frederick Warne Activity Book, 1886.

Greenberg, Jan and Sandra Jordan. *The Painter's Eye: Learning to Look at Contemporary American Art*. New York: Delacorte Press, 1991.

Greenfeld, Howard. *Marc Chagall*. New York: Harry N. Abrams, Inc., 1981.

Grimm, The Brothers. *Grimms' Fairy Tales*. Trans. E.V. Lucas, Lucy Crane, and Marian Edwardes. New York: Grosset & Dunlap. 1955.

Gubok, Shirley. *The Art of the Eskimo*. New York: Harper & Row, 1964.

Hamilton, Edith. *Mythology*. Boston: Little, Brown & Co., 1942.

Handel, George Frederic. *The Music for the Royal Fireworks*. (The Royal Philharmonic Orchestra, Yehudi Menuhin conducting. MCA Classics recording.)

Handforth, Thomas. *Mei Lei*. New York: Doubleday. 1990.

Harley, Rex. *Mary's Tiger*. New York: Harcourt Brace Jovanovich, 1990.

Heide, Florence Parry & Judith Heide Gilliland. *The Day of Ahmed's Secret*. New York: Lothrop, Lee & Shepard Books, 1990.

Helldorfer, M.C. *The Mapmaker's Daughter*. New York: Bradbury Press, 1991.

Heller, Ruth. *Animals Born Alive and Well*. New York: G.P. Putnam's Sons, 1982; *A Cache of Jewels and Other Collective Nouns*. New York: G.P. Putnam's Sons, 1987; *Chickens Aren't the Only Ones*. New York: G.P. Putnam's Sons, 1981; *Egyptian Cinderella* see Climo; *Kites Sail High: A Book about Verbs*. New York: Grosset & Dunlap, 1989; *Many Luscious Lollipops: A Book about Adjectives*. New York: Grosset & Dunlap, 1989; *Merry-Go-Round: A Books about Nouns*. New York: Grosset & Dunlap, 1990; *Plants That Never Ever Bloom*. New York: G.P. Putnam's Sons, 1984; *The Reasons for a Flower*. New York: Grosset & Dunlap, 1983.

Heyer, Marilee. *The Forbidden Door*. New York: Viking Kestrel, 1988.

Hillman, Lawrence E. *Nature Puzzlers*. Englewood, Colo.: Libraries Unlimited, 1989.

Hindle, Lee J. *Dragon Fall*. New York: Avon Books, 1984.

Hine, Al, and John Alcorn. *A Letter to Anywhere*. New York: Harcourt Brace & World, 1965.

Hissey, Jane. *Old Bear*. New York: Philomel Books, 1986.

Hobbs, Will. *Bearstone*. New York: Atheneum, 1989; *Changes in Latitudes*. New York: Atheneum, 1988; *Downriver*. New York: Atheneum, 1991.

Holme, Bryan (compiler). *Bulfinche's Mythology: The Greek and RomanFables Illustrated.* New York: The Viking Press, 1979.

Homer. Emil V. Rieu (translator). *The Illiad.* New York: Penguin, 1950.

Hooks, William H. *The Ballad of Belle Dorcas.* New York: Alfred A. Knopf, 1990.

Houston, James. *Akavak.* New York: Harcourt, Brace & World, 1968; *The White Archer.* New York: Harcourt, Brace & World, 1967; *Wolf Run.* New York: Harcourt, Brace & World, 1971.

Howe, James. *I Wish I Were a Butterfly.* New York: Harcourt Brace Jovanovich, Publishers, 1987.

Hubbard, Woodleigh. *C Is for Curious.* San Francisco, CA: Chronicle Books, 1990.

Hunt, Jonathan. *Illuminations.* New York: Bradbury Press, 1989.

Hutton, Warwick. *Theseus and the Minotaur.* New York: Margaret K. McElderry Books, 1989.

Inkpen, Mick. *The Blue Balloon.* Boston, MA: Little, Brown, 1989.

Irving, Jan. *Fanfares: Programs for Classrooms and Libraries.* Englewood, Colo.: Libraries Unlimited, 1990.

Irving, Washington. *Old Christmas.* New York: W. H. Smith Publishers, 1979 (reprint of 1894 edition).

Janeczko, Paul B. *The Music of What Happens: Poems that Tell Stories.* New York: Orchard Books, 1988.

Johnson, Tony and Tomie dePaola. *The Quilt Story.* New York: G.P. Putnam's, 1985.

Johnston, Tony. *The Badger and the Magic Fan.* New York: G.P.Putnam's Sons, 1990.

Jonas, Ann. *The Quilt.* New York: Greenwillow Books, 1984; *The Trek.* New York: Mulberry Books, 1985.

Kempadoo, Manghanita. *Letters of Thanks: A Christmas Tale.* New York: Simon & Schuster, 1969.

Kinsey-Warnock, Natalie. *The Canada Geese Quilt.* New York: Cobblehill Books/Dutton, 1989.

Koci, Marta. *Sarah's Bear.* Natick, MA:Picture Books Studio, 1987.

Lang, Andrew. *The Red Fairy Book.* Philadelphia: The John C. Winston Co. 1930.

Lang, H. Jack, ed. *Letters in American History: Words to Remember.* Cleveland, OH: Harmony Books, 1982.

Lasker, Joe. *A Tournament of Knights.* New York: Harper & Row, 1986; *Merry Ever After: The Story of Two Medieval Weddings.* New York: Puffin Books, 1978.

Lauber, Patricia. *Volcano: The Eruption and Healing of Mount St. Helens.* New York: Bradbury Press, 1986.

Laughlin, Mildred Knight, and Kathy Howard Latrobe. *Readers Theatre for Children.* Englewood, CO: Libraries Unlimited, 1990.

Leaf, Margaret. *Eyes of the Dragon.* New York: Lothrop, Lee & Shepard Books, 1987.

Lear, Edward. *The Owl and the Pussycat.* New York: G. P. Putnam's Sons, 1991.

Lester, Helen. *A Porcupine Named Fluffy.* Boston: Houghton Mifflin Company, 1989; *It Wasn't My Fault.* Boston: Houghton Mifflin Company, 1989; *Pookins Gets Her Way.* Boston: Houghton Mifflin Company, 1987; *Tacky the Penguin.* Boston: Houghton Mifflin Company, 1988; *The Wizard, the Fairy, and the Magic Chicken.* Boston: Houghton Mifflin Company, 1988.

Levinson, Riki. *Watch the Stars Come Out.* New York: E. P. Dutton, 1985.

Lewis, Elizabeth Foreman. *Young Fu of the Upper Yangtze.* New York: Henry Holt and Company, 1932.

Lionni, Leo. *Matthew's Dream.* New York: Alfred A. Knopf, 1991.

Lipsyte, Robert. *Assignment: Sports.* New York: Harper & Row Junior Books, 1984; *Free to Be Muhammad Ali.* New York: Harper & Row Junior Books, 1978; *Jock and Jill.* New York: Harper & Row Junior Books, 1982; *One Fat Summer.* New York: Bantam, 1984; *Summer Rules.* New York: Harper & Row Junior Books, 1981; *The Brave.* New York: Harper Collins Children's Books, 1991; *The Contender.* New York: Harper & Row Junior Books, 1967; *The Summerboy.* New York: Bantam, 1984; *The Young Artist.* New York: Dial Books, 1989.

Lopes, Sal. *The Wall: Images and Offerings from the Vietnam Veterans Memorial.* New York: Collins, Publishers, Inc., 1987.

Lyon, George Ella. *A B Cedar: An Alphabet of Trees.* New York: Orchard Books, 1989.

MacGill-Callahan, Sheila. *And Still the Turtle Watched.* New York: Dial Books for Young Readers, 1991.

Macrorie, Ken. *The I-Search Paper.* New Jersey: Boyton Cook Pub., 1988.

Mahy, Margaret. *The Seven Chinese Brothers.* New York: Scholastic Inc., 1990.

Martin, Bill Jr. , and John Archambault. *Barn Dance.* New York: Henry Holt, 1986; *Chicka Chicka Boom boom.* New York: Simon & Schuster Books for Young Readers, 1989; *The Ghost-Eye Tree.* New York: Henry Holt, 1985; *Here Are My Hands:* New York: Henry Holt, 1985; *Knots on a Counting Rope.* New York: Henry Holt, 1987; *Listen to the Rain.* New York: Henry Holt, 1988; *Up and Down on the Merry-Go-Round.* New York: Henry Holt, 1985; *White Dynamite and the Curly Kidd.* New York: Henry Holt, 1986.

Martin, Bill Jr. *Brown Bear, Brown Bear, What Do You See?* New York: Henry Holt, 1983.

Mason, Laura. *A Books of Boxes.* New York: Simon & Schuster Books for Young Readers, 1989.

Mathis, Sharon Bell. *The Hundred Penny Box.* New York: Puffin Books, 1975.

Mayer, Mercer. *Just Grandpa and Me.* New York: A Golden Book, 1985; *There's a Nightmare in My Closet.* New York: Dial Books for Young Readers, 1990 (a big book); *There's Something in My Attic.* New York: Dial Books for Young Readers, 1988.

Mayers, Florence Cassen. *ABC: The Wild West Buffalo Bill Historical Center, Cody, Wyoming.* New York: Harry N. Abrams, 1990.

Mayhew, James. *Katie's Picture Show.* New York: Bantam, 1989.

McDermott, Gerald. *Arrow to the Sun.* New York: Puffin Books, 1974.

McElmeel, Sharron L. *An Author A Month (for Pennies).* Englewood, Colo.:Libraries Unlimited, 1988; *Bookpeople: A First Album.* Englewood, Colo.: Libraries Unlimited, 1990.

McKee, David. *Elmer.* New York: Lothrop, Lee & Shepard Books, 1968.

McLanathan, Richard. *Leonardo da Vinci.* New York: Harry N. Abrams, Inc., 1991.

McLean, Margaret. *Make Your Own Musical Instruments.* Minneapolis, Lerner Publications Company, 1988.

McPhail, David. *Sisters.* New York: Harcourt Brace Jovanovich, 1984; *The Bear's Toothache.* Boston, MA: Joy Street Books, 1988; *First Flight.* Boston, MA: Little, Brown, 1987; *Fix-It.* New York: E.P. Dutton, 1984.

Melville, Herman. *Moby Dick.* New York: Bantam, 1981.

Meryman, Richard. *First Impressions: Andrew Wyeth.* New York: Harry N. Abrams, Inc., 1991.

Meyer, Carolyn. Eskimos: *Growing Up in a Changing Culture.* New York: Atheneum, 1977.

Meyer, Susan E. *Mary Cassatt.* New York: Harry N. Abrams, Inc., 1990.

Miles, Miska. *Annie and the Old One.* Boston: Little, Brown and Company, 1971.

Milne, A.A. *The House at Pooh Corner.* New York: E.P. Dutton, 1988; *Winnie the Pooh.* New York: Dutton, 1961, 1988.

Milord, Susan. *Adventures in Art.* Charlotte, Vermont: Williamson Publishing,1990.

Minarik, Else H. *Little Bear.* New York: Harper & Row, 1978.

Monjo, F.M. *Letters to Horseface: Being the Story of Wolfgang Amadeus Mozart's Journey to Italy, 1769-1770, When He Was a Boy of Fourteen.* New York: Viking Press, 1975.

Mudd, Maria M. *The Butterfly.* New York:Stewart, Tabori & Chang, Inc., 1991.

Myers, Robert Manson, ed. *The Children of Pride.* New Haven, CT: Yale University Press, 1972.

National Film Board of Canada, 680 Fifth Avenue, New York, NY 10019.

Neumeier, Marty, and Byron Glaser. *Action Alphabet.* New York: Greenwillow Books, 1985.

Nixon, Joan Lowery. *Secret, Silent Screams.* New York: Delacorte Press, 1988; *The Orphan Train Quartet.* New York: Bantam, 1987.

Noble, Trinka Hakes. *The Day Jimmy's Boa Ate the Wash.* New York: Dial Books for Young Readers, 1980; *Jimmy's Boa and the Big Splash Birthday Bash.* New York: Dial Books for Young Readers, 1989.

Norman, Howard. *The Owl-Scatterer.* New York: The Atlantic Monthly Press,1986.

Nye, Naomi Shihab. *This Same Sky: A Collection of Poems from around the World.* New York: Four Winds Press, 1992.

O'Dell, Scott. *Alexandra.* New York: Fawcett, 1985; *Black Star, Bright Dawn.* Boston, Houghton Mifflin Company, 1988; *The Black Pearl.* Boston: Houghton Mifflin Company, 1988; *Carlotta.* Boston, Houghton Mifflin Company, 1977; *Dark Canoe.* Boston, Houghton Mifflin Company, 1968; *Island of the Blue Dolphins.* New York: Dell, 1987; *Sarah Bishop.* Boston, Houghton Mifflin Company, 1980; *Sing Down the Moon.* Boston, Houghton Mifflin Company, 1970; *Streams to the River, River to the Sea: A Novel of Sacagawea.* Boston: Houghton Mifflin Company, 1986; *The Amethyst Ring.* Boston, Houghton Mifflin Company, 1983; *The Captive.* Boston, Houghton Mifflin Company, 1979; *The Castle in the Sea.* Boston, Houghton Mifflin Company, 1983; *The Cruise of the Arctic Star.* Boston, Houghton Mifflin Company, 1973; *The Feathered Serpent.* Boston, Houghton Mifflin Company, 1981; *The Spanish Smile.* Boston, Houghton Mifflin Company, 1982; *Zia.* Boston, Houghton Mifflin Company, 1976.

Ovid. A. D. Melville (translator). *Metamorphoses.* New York: Oxford U. Press, 1987.

Pappas, Theoni. *Math Talk: Mathematical Ideas in Poems for Two Voices.* New York: Wide World Publishing/Tetra, 1990.

Parkinson, Kathy. *The Farmer in the Dell.* Morton Grove, Illinois: Albert Whitman, 1988.

Parks, Brenda, and Judith Smith. *The Enormous Watermelon.* Crystal Lake, IL: Rigby, 1986 (reprinted 1989).

Paterson, Katherine. *Bridge to Terabithia.* New York: Crowell Company, 1977; *Gates of Excellence: On Reading and Writing Books for Children.* New York: E.P. Dutton, 1981; *The Great Gilly Hopkins.* New York: Harper and Row Jr. Books, 1978; *The Spying Heart: More Thoughts on Reading and Writing Books for Children.* New York: E.P. Dutton, 1989; *The Tale of the Mandarin Ducks.* New York: LodestarBooks, 1990.

Patterson, Geoffrey. *The Lion and the Gypsy.* New York: Doubleday, 1990.

Paul, Ann Whitford. *Eight Hands Round: A Patchwork Alphabet.* New York: Harper Collins Publishers, 1991.

Paulsen, Gary. *Brain's Winter.* New York: Delacorte Press 1996; *Canyons.* New York: Delacorte Press, 1990; *Dancing Carl.* New York: Penguin, 1987; *Dogsong.* New York: Bradbury Press, 1985;. *Hatchet.* New York: Bradbury Press, 1987; *Popcorn Days & Buttermilk Nights.* New York: Penguin, 1989;. *Sentries.* New York: Penguin, 1987; *The Boy Who Owned the School.* New York: Orchard Books, 1990; *The Cookcamp.* New York: Orchard Books, 1991; *The Crossing.* New York: Orchard Books, 1987; *The Island.* New York: Orchard Books, 1988;. *The Night the White Deer Died.* New York: Delacorte Press, 1978; *The Voyage of the Frog.* New York: Orchard Books, 1989;. *The Winter Room.* New York: Orchard Books, 1989;. *Tracker.* New York: Penguin, 1987;. *Wood-Song.* New York: Bradbury Press, 1990.

Perlutsky, Jack. *Something Big Has Been Here.* New York: Greenwillow Books, 1990.

Pinkwater, Daniel. *Aunt Lulu.* New York: Aladdin Books, 1991.

Polacco, Patricia. *Babushka's Doll.* New York: Simon and Schuster Books, 1990;. *Boatride with Lillian Two-Blossom.* New York: Philomel Books, 1988;. *I Can Hear the Sun.* New York: Philomel Books, 1996; *Just Plain Fancy.* New York: Bantam, 1990; *Meteor.* New York: Philomel Books, 1987; *Rechenka's Eggs.* New York: Philomel Books, 1988; *The Keeping Quilt.* New York: Simon & Schuster, 1988; *Thunder Cake.* New York: Philomel Books, 1990.

Precek, Katharine Wilson. *Penny in the Road.* New York: Macmillan Publishing Company, 1989.

Provensen, Alice. *The Buck Stops Here: The Presidents of the United States.* New York: Harper & Row, Publishers, 1990.

Purdy, Susan and Cass R. Sandak. *Eskimos: A Civilization Project Book.* New York: Franklin Watts, 1982.

Rae, Mary M. *The Farmer in the Dell: A Singing Game.* New York: Viking, 1988.

Raffi. *The Raffi Singable Songs Collection.* Hollywood, CA: A&M Records, Inc., 1988.

Rasmussen, Knud. *Beyond the High Hills/A Book of Eskimo Poems.* Cleveland, Ohio: World Publishing Co., 1961.

Rice, James. *La Nochebuena South of the Border.* Gretna, Louisiana: Pelican Publishing Company, 1993.

Ringgold, Faith. *Tar Beach.* New York: Crown Publishers, Inc., 1991.

Root, Phyllis. *Moon Tiger.* New York: Henry Holt and Company, 1985.

San Souci, Robert D. *The Enchanted Tapestry.* New York: Dial Books for Young Readers, 1987.

Sandburg, Carl. *Abraham Lincoln: The Prarie Years and the War Years.* New York: Harcourt Brace Jovanovich, 1974; *Arithmetic.* New York: Harcourt Brace Jovanovich, Publishers, 1978,1993.

Savriencka

Say, Allen. *The Bicycle Man.* Boston, Massachusetts: Houghton Mifflin Company, 1982.

Seeley, Laura L. *The Books of Shadowboxes: The Story of the ABC's.* Atlanta, GA: Peachtree Publishers, 1990.

Sendak, Maurice. *We Are All in the Dumps,* New York: Harper Collins, 1993; *Where the Wild Things Are.* New York: Harper & Row, Publishers, 1984.

Shakespeare, William. *A Midsummer Night's Dream.* New Haven, Conn.: Yale University Press, 1965; *Macbeth,* New Haven, Conn.: Yale University Press, 1965; *The Most Excellent andLamentable Tragedy of Romeo and Juliet.* New Haven, Conn.: Yale University Press, 1965; *The Merchant of Venice,* New Haven, Conn.: Yale University Press, 1965.

Shannon, George. *Stories to Solve: folktales from Around the World.* New York: Greenwillow Books, 1985.

Sharmat, Marjorie Weinman. *I'm Terrific.* New York: Scholastic, 1977; *I'm The Best!* New York: Holiday House, 1991.

Shaw, Nancy. *Sheep in a Jeep.* Boston, MA: Houghton Mifflin Company, 1986.

Siegel, Beatrice. *Sam Ellis's Island.* New York: Four Winds Press, 1985.

Sills, Leslie. *Inspirations: Stories About Women Artists.* Niles, Illinois: Albert Whitman & Company, 1989.

Silverstein, Shel. *Where the Sidewalk Ends.* New York: Harper and Row, 1974,

Slator, Teddy. *Molly's Monsters.* New York: Platt & Munk, 1988.

Smith, Ron. *Mythologies of the World: A Guide to Sources.* Urbana, Illinois:National Council of Teachers of English, 1981.

Sneve, Virginia Driving Hawk, ed. *Dancing Teepees: Poems of American Indian Youth.* Illustrated by Stephen Gammell. New York: Holiday House, 1989.

Snyder, Dianne. *The Boy of the Three-Year Nap.* Boston: Houghton-Mifflin Company, 1988.

Sobol, Donald, *Encyclopedia Brown Saves the Day. No. 7.* New York: Bantam,1989;. *Encyclopedia Brown & the Case of the Secret Pitch. No. 2.*New York: Bantam,1965; *Encyclopedia Brown and the Case of the Disgusting Sneakers. No. 18* New York: Bantam,1990; *Encyclopedia Brown and the Case of the Midnight Visitor. No. 13.* New York: Bantam, 1977; *Encyclopedia Brown and the Case of the Treasure Hunt. No. 17.* New York: Bantam, 1989; *Encyclopedia Brown and the Mysterious Handprints. No. 16.* New York: Bantam, 1986; *Encyclopedia Brown Boy Detective. No. 1.* New York: Bantam, 1978,1963; *Encyclopedia Brown Finds the Clue. No. 3.* New York: Bantam, 1965; *Encyclopedia Brown Gets His Man. No. 4.* New York: Bantam, 1967; *Encyclopedia Brown Keeps the Peace. No. 6.*.New York: Bantam, 1973; *Encyclopedia Brown Shows the Way. No. 9.*.New York: Bantam, 1972; *Encyclopedia Brown Takes the Case. No. 10.*.New York: Bantam, 1973; *Encyclopedia Brown Tracks Them Down. No. 8.*.New York: Bantam, 1971.

Soto, Gary. *A Fire in My Hands.* Scholastic Inc., 1990;. *A Summer Life.* New York: Laurel-Leaf, 1990;. *Baseball in April and Other Stories.* New York: Harcourt, Brace Jovanovich, 1990;. *Taking Sides.* New York: Harcourt, Brace Jovanovich, 1991; *The Bike* (film). Att: Rosa Johnson, Chicano Studies, 3404 Dwinelle Hall, University of California at Berkeley, Berkeley, CA;. *Neighborhood Odes.* New York: Harcourt Brace Jovanovich, 1992; *Who Will Know Us? New Poems.* San Francisco: Chronicle Books, 1990.

Spinelli, Eileen. *Somebody Loves You Mr. Hatch.* New York: Bradbury Press, 1991.

Spinelli, Jerry. *Dump Days.* Boston: Little, Brown and Company, 1988;. *Jason & Marceline.* Boston: Little, Brown and Company, 1986;. *Maniac Magee.* Boston: Little, Brown and Company, 1990;. *Space Station Seventh Grade.* Boston: Little, Brown and Company, 1982;. *The Night of the Whale.* New York: Dell, 1988; *Who Put That Hair in My Toothbrush?* Boston: Little, Brown and Company, 1984.

Steig, William. *Abel's Island.* New York: Farrar, Straus & Giroux, 1985; *Amos & Boris.* New York: Puffin Books, 1986; *Brave Irene.* New York: Farrar, Straus & Giroux, 1986; *CDB* . New York: Farrar, Straus & Giroux, 1984; *Doctor DeSoto.* New York: Farrar, Straus and Giroux, 1982; *Dominic.* New York: Farrar, Straus & Giroux, 1984; *Farmer Palmer's Wagon Ride.* New York: Farrar, Straus & Giroux, 1974; *Gorky Rises.* New York: Farrar, Straus & Giroux, 1986; *Roland the Minstrel Pig.* New York: Farrar, Straus & Giroux, 1968; *Solomon the Rusty Nail* . New York: Farrar, Straus & Giroux, 1985; *Spinky Sulkes.* New York: Farrar, Straus & Giroux, 1988; *The Amazing Bone.* New York: Farrar, Straus & Giroux, 1976; *The Real Thief* New York: Farrar, Straus & Giroux, 1984; *The Zabajaba Jungle.* New York: Farrar, Straus & Giroux, 1987; *Tiffky Doofky.* New York: Farrar, Straus & Giroux, 1987; *Yellow and Pink.* New York: Farrar, Straus & Giroux, 1988; *Sylvester and the Magic Pebble.* New York: Simon and Schuster, 1969.

Strand, Mark. *Rembrandt takes a Walk.* New York: Clarkson N. Potter, Inc. 1986.

Thompson, . *City Kids in China.* New York: Harper Collins Children Books, 1991.

Thurber, James. *Many Moons.* New York: Harcourt Brace Jovanovich, Publishers, 1945 text copyright (renewed in 1970), 1990.

Titherington, Jeanne. *Pumpkin Pumpkin.* New York: Greenwillow Books, 1986.

Trimble, Stephen. *The Village of Blue Stone.* New York: Macmillan Publishing Company, 1990.

Turkle, Brinton. *Deep in the Forest.* New York: E.P. Dutton, 1976; *Do Not Open.* New York: E. P. Dutton, 1981.

Van Allsburg, Chris. *The Z Was Zapped.* Boston, MA: Houghton Mifflin, 1987.

Van Buren, Abigail. *The Best of Dear Abby.* Kansas City, MO: Andrews & McMeel, 1989.

Venezia, Mike. *Mary Cassatt*. Chicago: Childrens Press, 1989.

Viorst, Judith. *Alexander and the Terrible, Horrible, No Good, Very Bad Day*. New York: Atheneum, 1976; *Alexander, Who Used to Be Rich Last Sunday*. New York: Atheneum, 1978; *Earrings!* New York: Atheneum, 1990; *I'll Fix Anthony*. New York: Harper & Row, 1969; *If I Were in Charge of the World and Other Worries*. New York: Aladdin Books, 1981; *My Mama Says There Aren't Any Zombies, Ghosts, Vampires, Creatures, Demons, Monsters, Fiends, Goblins, or Things*. New York: Atheneum, 1973; *Rosie and Michael*. New York: Atheneum, 1974; *Sunday Morning*. New York: Harper & Row, 1968; *The Good-Bye Book*. New York: Atheneum, 1988; *The Tenth Good Thing about Barney*. New York: Atheneum, 1975.

Von Hassell, Ulrich. *The Von Hassell Diaries, 1938-1944: The Story of the Forces Against Hitler Inside Germany*. New York: AMS Press, 1947.

Vrbova, Zuza. *Volcanoes and Earthquakes*. Mahwah, NJ: Troll Associates, 1990.

Waber, Bernard. *Ira Sleeps Over*. Boston, MA: Houghton Mifflin, 1972.

Warner, Gertrude C. *Benny Uncovers a Mystery*. Niles, Illinois: Albert Whitman & Company, 1976; *Blue Bay Mystery*. Niles, Illinois: Albert Whitman & Company, 1960; *Bus Station Mystery*. Niles, Illinois: Albert Whitman & Company, 1974; *Caboose Mystery*. Niles, Illinois: Albert Whitman & Company, 1966; *Mike's Mystery*. Niles, Illinois: Albert Whitman & Company, 1960; *Mountain Top Mystery*. Niles, Illinois: Albert Whitman & Company, 1964; *Mystery Behind the Wall*. Niles, Illinois: Albert Whitman & Company, 1973; *Mystery in the Sand*. Niles, Illinois: Albert Whitman & Company, 1971; *Mystery Ranch*. Niles, Illinois: Albert Whitman & Company, 1958; *Schoolhouse Mystery*. Niles, Illinois: Albert Whitman & Company, 1965; *Surprise Island*. Niles, Illinois: Albert Whitman & Company, 1956; *The Lighthouse Mystery*. Niles, Illinois: Albert Whitman & Company, 1963; *The Woodshed Mystery*. Niles, Illinois: Albert Whitman & Company, 1962; *The Yellow House Mystery*. Niles, Illinois: Albert Whitman & Company, 1957; *The Boxcar Children*. Niles, Illinois: Albert Whitman & Company,1977

White, Alana. *Come Next Spring*. New York: Clarion Books, l990.

Whittington, Mary K. *The Patchwork Lady*. New York: Harcourt Brace Jovanovich, 1991.

Williams, Terry Tempest and Ted Major. *The Secret Language of Snow*. San Francisco, CA: Sierra Club/Pantheon Books, 1984.

Williams, William Carlos. *Pictures from Brueghel and Other Poems*. New York: New Directions Books, 1962.

Wilson, Edward E. "Autumnal Equinox" in *The Music of What Happens: Poems that Tell Stories*. Selected by Paul B. Janeczko. New York: Orchard Books, 1988, "Shielding the Basic Student," *English in Texas*, Vol. 14, No1. 3, 1983, pp. 43-47.

Winthrop, Elizabeth. *Lizzie and Harold*. New York: Lothrop, Lee & Shepard Books, 1986.

Wolfe, Thomas. *The Web and the Rock*. New York: Harper & Row, 1986; *You Can't Go Home Again*. New York: Harper & Row, 1973.

Wood, Audrey. *The Napping House*. New York: Harcourt Brace Jovanovich, Publishers, 1984.

Woodruff, Elvira. *The Wing Shop*. New York: Holiday House, 1991.

Yabuuchi, Masayuki. *Whose Footprints?* New York: Philomel Books, 1985.

Yagawa, Sumiko (translated by Katherine Paterson). *The Crane Wife*. New York: Mulberry Books, 1979 (English copyright 1981).

Yep, Laurence. *Child of the Owl*. New York: Harper & Row, 1977; *Dragon of the Lost Sea*. New York: Harper & Row, 1982; *Dragon Steel*. New York: Harper & Row, 1985; *Dragonwings*. New York: Harper & Row, 1975; *Kind Hearts & Gentle Monsters*. New York: Harper & Row, 1982; *Mountain Light*. New York: Harper & Row, 1985; *Sweetwater*. New York: Harper & Row, 1983; *The Mark Twain Murders*. New York: Macmillan, 1982; *The Rainbow People*. New York: Harper & Row, 1985; *The Serpent's Children*. New York: Harper & Row, 1984.

Yolen, Jane. *Owl Moon*. New York: Philomel Books, 1987; *Sky Dogs*. New York: Harcourt Brace Jovanovich, Publishers, 1990; *Wings*. New York: Harcourt Brace Jovanovich, Publishers, 1991.

Yue, Charlotte and David. *The Igloo*. Boston: Houghton Mifflin, 1988.

Zadrzynska, Ewa. *The Girl with a Watering Can*. New York: Chameleon Books, Inc., 1990.

Ziefert, Harriet, and Mavis Smith. *In a Scary Old House*. New York: Puffin Books, 1989.

Zinsser, William. *Inventing the Truth*. Boston: Houghton Mifflin Company. 1987.

Zuromskis, Diane (Illustrator). *The Farmer in the Dell*. Boston: Little, Brown and Company, 1978.

Acknowledgements

The author and publisher wishes to thank the following publishers for permission to reprint the covers of their books.

Albert Whitman & Company
Cover art by Charles Tang of Boxcar Children® Mystery # 1, *The Boxcar Children* by Gertrude Chandler Warner is reprinted with permission from the publisher Albert Whitman & Company, Morton Grove, Illinois, © 1942.
Alfred A. Knopf, Inc.
Cover art by Brian Pinkney, *The Ballad of Belle Dorcas* by William H. Hooks is reprinted with permission from the publisher Alfred A. Knoft, Inc., New York, © 1990.
Bantam Doubleday Dell
Cover art by Leonard Shortall, *Enclycolpedia Brown* by Donald J. Sobol is reprinted with permission from the publisher Bantam Doubleday Dell, New York, © 1963.
Cover art by Robert Vickery, *I am the cheese* by Robert Cormier is reprinted with permission from the publisher Bantam Doubleday Dell, New York, © 1977.
Cover art by Leonoard Weisgard, *Hailstone and halibut bones* by Mary O'Neil is reprinted with permission from the publisher Bantam Doubleday Dell, Inc., New York, © 1961.
Cover art by Robert Vickery, *I am the cheese* by Robert Cormier is reprinted with permission from the publisher Bantam Doubleday Dell, New York, © 1977.
Farrar, Straus, & Giroux, Inc.
Copyright © 1975 by Natalie Babbitt. Reprinted by permission of the publisher, Farrar, Straus and Giroux.
G.P. Putnam's Sons
Cover art by Tomie dePaola, *The Art Lesson* by Tomie dePaola is reprinted with permission from the publisher G.P. Putnam's Sons , New York, © 1989.
Cover art by Tomie dePaola, *Tomie dePaola's Book of Poems* by Tomie dePaola is reprinted with permission from the publisher G.P. Putnam's Sons , New York, © 1988.
Cover art by John Schoenherr, *Owl Moon* by Jane Yolan is reprinted with permission from the publisher G.P. Putnam's Sons , New York, © 1987.
Harcourt Brace and Company (HBJ)
Cover art from *Arithmetic* by Carl Sandburg, illustrations copyright ©1993 by Ted Rand, reproduced by permission of Harcourt Brace & Company.
Cover art from *Easting the Alphabet: Fruit and Vegetables from A to Z* , copyright ©198 by Lois Ehlert, reproduced by permission of Harcourt Brace & Company.
Cover art from *I Wish I Were a Butterfly* by James Howe, illustration copyright ©1987 by Ed Young, reproduced by permission of Harcourt Brace & Company.
Cover art from *The Magic Fan,* copyright ©1989 by Keith Baker, reproduced by permission of Harcourt Brace & Company.
Cover art from *The Napping House* by Audrey Wood, illustrations copyright ©1984 by Don Wood, reproduced by permission of Harcourt Brace & Company.
Cover art from *Neighborhood Odes* by Gary Soto, illustrations by David Diaz copyright ©1992 Harcourt Brace & Company, reproduced by permission of the publisher.
Cover art from *Taking Sides* by Gary Soto, illustrations copyright ©1991 by Alan MAzzetti, reproduced by permission of Harcourt Brace & Company.
Cover art from *Wings* by Jane Yolen, illustrations copyright ©1991 by Dennis Nolan, reproduced by permission of Harcourt Brace & Company.
Harper Collins Publisher
Cover art by Ed Acuna, *The Brave* by Robert Lipsyte is reprinted with permission from the publisher Harper Collins Publisher, New York, © 1991.
William Morris at Harper Collins Publisher
Cover art by Donna Diamond, *Bridge to Terabithia* by Katherine Paterson is reprinted with permission from the publisher Harper Collins Publisher, New York, © 1977.
Cover art by Ronald Himler, *Dragonwings* by Laurence Yep is reprinted with permission from the publisher Harper Collins Publisher, New York, © 1975.
Cover art by Leonard Weigard, *The Important Book* by Margaret Wise Brown is reprinted with permission from the publisher Harper Collins Publisher, New York, © 1949.
Cover art by Carol Palmer, *Maniac Magee* by Jerry Spinelli is reprinted with permission from the publisher Harper Collins Publisher, New York, © 1990.
Cover art by Aliki, *A Medieval Feast* by Aliki is reprinted with permission from the publisher Harper Collins Publisher, New York, © 1983.
Cover art by Shel Silverstein, *Where the Sidewalk Ends* by Shel Silverstein is reprinted with permission from the pub-

ABOUT THE AUTHOR

Joyce Armstrong Carroll, Ed.D., has taught almost all grades from elementary to graduate school in her thirty-nine years in the profession. An avid reader and prolific writer, she has published over fifty articles and poems as well as co-authoring *Acts of Teaching: How to Teach Writing* with Edward E. Wilson. She also co-authored *Jesus Didn't Use Worksheets: A 2000-Year-Old Model for Good Teaching* with theologian Ron Habermas. She co-edited with Edward E. Wilson *Poetry After Lunch: Poems to Read Aloud,* a 1998 winner of ALA Best Books for Young Adults and the New York Public Library's Best Books for the Teen Age 1998. Additionally, she has written the five-book Dr. JAC series, the best of which is now published under the title *The Best of Dr. JAC.* Her most recent book, forthcoming May, 1998, is titled *Phonics Friendly Books: Teaching Phonics through Children's Literature.*

As director of the New Jersey Writing Project in Texas, she enjoys the privilege of training teachers and teaching students across the state of Texas, as well as in Florida and Oklahoma. She lives with her husband.